JME Publishing
San Diego, California
smartclassroommanagement.com

Printed in the U.S.A.

Many thanks to:
Christine Haack
Lucy Goodwin
Mike McKown

Design by:
Ben Morris

I.S.B.N. 978-1-889236-27-8

The Classroom Management Secret

And 45 Other Keys to
a Well-Behaved Class

MICHAEL LINSIN

Contents

"...as my eyes grew accustomed to the light, details of the room within emerged slowly from the mist, strange animals, statues, and gold—everywhere the glint of gold. For the moment—an eternity it must have seemed to the others standing by—I was struck dumb with amazement, and when Lord Carnarvon, unable to stand the suspense any longer, inquired anxiously, 'Can you see anything?' it was all I could do to get out the words, 'Yes, wonderful things.'"

-Howard Carter, *Tomb of Tutankhamen*

1

The Classroom Management Secret

♀

THE SECRET you are about to learn will forever change the way you manage your classroom. That is my hope, anyway, and my strongest belief. For I am convinced that it holds the keys to a well-behaved classroom, a deeply fulfilling career, and an ability to impact your students for a lifetime.

I first learned of this secret more than 30 years ago from Bill Heyde, my high school English teacher. I was a bored and reluctant student whose heart for learning was transformed and then set afire while sitting in Bill's class.

Bill didn't teach me this secret so explicitly, however. It was the example he set, the learning environment he created, and the profound implications they had on my life that informed my ideas about classroom management. I entered Bill's classroom one person . . . and walked out four years later someone entirely different. So changed by the experience that my greatest aspiration was to do what he did and answer the high calling to be a teacher.

The secret is made up of two distinct principles often viewed as being on opposite ends of the classroom management spectrum. It is elegantly simple, easy to understand, and available to anyone wanting to avail themselves of its power. So what is this secret?

I define it this way:

The Classroom Management Secret

★ It is creating a classroom your students love being part of combined with an unwavering commitment to accountability.

Precisely what this looks like, why it's so effective, and how you can do it yourself forms the rest of this book. First published as individual blog posts at smartclassroommanagement.com, the subsequent 45 strategies will challenge your assumptions, excite your heart with possibility, and provide you with the tools to be the teacher your students will always remember.

Although each strategy stands alone in its effectiveness, they are meant to work together and thus are arranged intentionally to allow for deeper understanding. They unfold one theme, one idea, and one solution at a time, building one atop the other and bringing the secret into sharp focus.

As you read through the strategies, you'll notice that the welfare and development of students comes first. You'll find no trickery, no manipulation, and no hurtful methods. What you will find are honest strategies that work, that any teacher can implement, and that are best for students.

Classroom management doesn't have to be complex. It doesn't have to be a daily battle. And you don't have to be the stern, stressed-out teacher you never wanted to become.

On the contrary, classroom management can be a source of joy and satisfaction. It can be life changing and perspective altering. It can be poignant and lovely and even beautiful. It can build relationships, teach lessons, and create memories that endure for a lifetime.

My sincerest hope is that the secret will do as much for you and your students as it has done for me and the many students I've had the privilege of teaching.

2

Why You Should Smile on the First Day of School

ę

YOU'VE LIKELY HEARD the oft-repeated recommendation that teachers should never smile the first three months of the school year. The idea being that if you show kindness toward your students, they'll see it as a weakness and take advantage of you.

Hogwash.

Although it's true students can and often do come to the conclusion that their teacher is a pushover, it has nothing to do with showing kindness. You're only a pushover if you don't do what you say you're going to do.

The truth is, smiling is a powerful classroom management strategy you should begin using the first day of school.

Here's why:

It sets the proper tone.

A smile is a subtle message that kindness and politeness are expected in your classroom. It starts a slow but sure chain of smiles that pay forward throughout your new class, setting a tone conducive to learning, behaving, and getting along with classmates.

The Classroom Management Secret

It's disarming.

Students are nervous on the first day of school, particularly those who are shy and take time adjusting to new surroundings. A smile puts them at ease. It tells them that everything is going to be okay, that they're right where they should be, and that their teacher is on their side.

It makes you more likable.

Your likability is crucial to effective classroom management and a smile is the simplest way to improve it. This doesn't mean you have to plaster an all-day grin on your face like a beauty contestant. Just be generous with your smile. Give it away freely, with no strings attached.

It builds rapport.

A smile on the first day of school is the first step toward building rapport with your students. Genuine, behavior-influencing rapport can only happen when students are drawn to you. It can never be forced upon them (or it will be repelled). A smile draws students in like bees to honey.

It makes a good first impression.

One of the problems with not smiling is that you'll spend months trying to overcome the bad first impression you've given your students. It's better to get them on your side and buying into your program right off the bat. Being warm and welcoming is a persuasive first step.

It makes your sky-high expectations palatable.

If you want impeccable behavior, then you have to ask for it, even demand it, of your students from the very beginning. When you smile on the first day of school, it makes your non-negotiable classroom management plan and the realization that *a lot* is expected go down easier.

It starts you on the right foot with parents.

Making a good first impression with parents is important, and the best way to do it is through their children. If a child comes home from school and tells her (or his) parents that she loves her new teacher and can't wait to go back the next day, then her parents are more likely to trust you, believe in you, and give you the benefit of the doubt.

It's a reminder.

Smiling is a reminder to savor the opportunity to teach another group of students. It reminds you to go about your first day with calm and graceful purpose, not taking the inevitable bumps in the road too seriously.

Effective Classroom Management Starts With A Smile

Today's students aren't intimidated by aloofness, awkward silence, or blank-faced detachment. These old-school methods merely make them unhappy to be in your classroom and more likely than ever to engage in misbehavior.

In this day and age, to effectively manage students you need to combine a near obsessive commitment to following your classroom management plan with an equal dedication to creating a learning environment your students like and enjoy coming to every day.

And it starts on the first day of school.

It starts, with a smile.

3

7 Keys to the First Day of School

THE FIRST DAY OF SCHOOL is about setting the tone. It's about focusing on the first wee little steps leading to the most memorable school year your students will ever have. There is no room for weak first impressions, no room for indecisiveness, and no room to leave your students bored or uninspired.

It's best to think of the first day of school as a microcosm of the coming year. In other words, it should represent who you are and what you want your classroom to be.

The seven keys below may not be the only items on your agenda, but in terms of making an impression on your students, they are the most important.

1. A smile.

It's so simple, but also so very important. A smile to greet your students is the first step to building rapport. It's the first step to creating a trusting, close-knit relationship with your new class. If your students like you and trust you, then classroom management becomes much easier. A smile activates instant likability—and so much more.

2. A peaceful pace.

Establish a peaceful pace to your classroom by speaking calmly but firmly, taking your time, pausing often, and never moving on until you get exactly what you want from your new students. These powerful strategies will begin grooving the initial learning and behaving habits that make for a mature, attentive classroom.

3. A routine.

With your new students eager to please, early the first morning is the perfect time to send the message that you expect excellence in everything they do, even the most mundane routines. Teach a highly detailed lesson on how to enter your classroom in the morning—or any other common routine. Be of good cheer, make it enjoyable and participatory, but set your expectations beyond anything they've ever experienced.

4. A story.

Storytelling is a powerful medium. Teachers who use it to their advantage—to communicate profound truths, fire imagination and wonder, awaken indifferent students, and more—are infinitely more effective. A fun or unusual anecdote about you, perhaps from your childhood, will initiate that first spark, that first inkling, that being in your classroom is going to be different, and somehow, some way, wonderfully special.

5. A plan.

Although you'll use the rest of the first week to teach your classroom management plan in depth, it's important to give an overview of your rules and consequences on the first day. The reason is twofold. First, your students need to know your boundaries so you can begin enforcing them. Second, it's an opportunity to express your deep commitment to protect their right to learn and enjoy school without interference.

6. A lesson.

Send the message that yours is a classroom of focused, get-down-to-it learning by jumping into academics on the first day—but not with just any lesson. Choose *one thing* you want your students to understand or know how to do, and teach the heck out of it. Show them something unique, something they haven't seen or experienced before. Be at your best, and they'll start the year excited about learning.

7. A little fun.

Show your students that your sky-high expectations extend beyond behavior and academics. To be in your classroom also means to have fun. Small doses of humor throughout the day, a getting-to-know-you activity, a simple openness to enjoying your students—any of these will do. The idea is to establish a classroom environment that balances hard work with camaraderie, friendship, and joy. In other words, a classroom they look forward to coming to every day.

SMOOTH SAILING AHEAD

It pays to make your first day of school a special one, to take advantage of your one chance to make a first impression, to leave your students exhilarated, out of breath, and happily shaken.

The Classroom Management Secret

You'll be immediately elevated to favorite-teacher status. Your students will be excited to come back the next day and inspired to please you with their best.

And parents? They will be thrilled and firmly ensconced in your corner.

But like a shrewd and grizzled sea captain, you have an ulterior motive. For you know that when you begin the journey with calm waters and a strong wind at your back . . .

It's smooth sailing ahead.

4

The Biggest First Day of School Mistake You Can Make

ᛦ

THERE IS A COMMON MISTAKE teachers make on the first day of school that sets in motion bad student habits and misbehaviors that can last the rest of the school year. That's a big statement, I know. But this one particular mistake will be responsible for scores of teachers getting off to a disastrous classroom management start—one many will never recover from.

What makes this mistake most troubling is its deviousness. You see, it's a sneaky little thing, harmless in appearance and barely noticeable, even to the most discerning professional eye. Most teachers won't even know they made a mistake, let alone one so spectacular, until weeks later when it hits them like a splash of cold water to the face.

And even then, they won't know what they did wrong.

It starts innocently.

Morning breaks on the first day of school, your new students arrive, and everything proceeds as planned. You model how you want them to enter the classroom. You lead them in a getting-to-know-you activity. Then you get down to the business of your classroom management plan.

Typical of a new group of students after a long summer break, they're attentive and respectful. And you're pleased with how things are going. By late afternoon all is well and rolling along according to plan. You were thorough with your behavior expectations, and they're following your rules as modeled. *Yes! This is going to be a great year.*

The end of the day nears. You review the evening's homework assignment and model how you want your students to gather backpacks, push in chairs, and line up quietly for dismissal. They nod their heads, all smiles. *I love my new class!*

A minute or so before the bell rings, you give your students the signal to begin the end-of-day procedure. In their exuberance, several students rush the door to line up. A few happily approach you like puppy dogs, wanting to share a story or two. A few more linger a moment at their desks, chatting with their tablemates.

You remind the runners to walk, tell the lingerers to get a move on, and banter a moment with the students who approached you. And as the bell rings you shoo them all out the door with a wave. *What an awesome day. What a great class!*

The door closes and you fall into your chair with a happy sigh, never realizing that you just made a colossal mistake, one that will cause your students to begin ignoring your directions, breaking your rules, and engaging in misbehavior.

It happens so fast.

So, did you catch it? Did you notice the mistake? The teacher in the above scenario was lulled into complacency by her (or his) students' good behavior. She was so thrilled with how well the first day was going that she dropped the ball during the final minute.

Her students didn't follow the end-of-day procedure as modeled, but because they weren't technically "misbehaving," she let it go. And this is where so many teachers who struggle with classroom management go wrong.

When you let things go, even seemingly innocent behaviors, it nudges a tiny speck of a snowball down a steep and bottomless hill. And the farther it gets down the hill, the more difficult it is to push it back up to the top.

Although the above scenario in and of itself is harmless, it sends a message to your students that you don't really mean what you say. And as soon as this germ of an idea gets in their heads, a host of bad things begin to happen. Your students will start tuning out the sound of your voice. They'll become inattentive and disrespectful. They won't follow directions well. And misbehavior will be a daily, even hourly, presence in your classroom.

In response you'll begin raising your voice to show your students that you really do mean it. You'll start pulling them aside for lectures, talking-tos, and finger-waggings. You'll grow frustrated. And your students will begin thinking that maybe you're not so nice after all.

It doesn't have to be this way.

That the students in the above scenario didn't line up for dismissal like the teacher asked was predictable. Students will test the waters, albeit gently, even on the first day of school. And when they do, it's an opportunity for you to teach a critical lesson—one that will reverberate long after the moment has passed.

The lesson is this: In our classroom, the expectation is that we do things the right way. We listen attentively. We follow directions. We pursue excellence in everything we do because excellence transfers from the simple and commonplace to more important things like scholarship, kindness, and respect.

With that in mind, let's rewind our scenario. As soon as the teacher notices that her students are not doing what was asked, she stops talking and stands in one place. She ignores the students approaching. She ignores the running. She ignores the students taking their sweet time to line-up. She just waits.

One by one, as the students begin to notice, they get quiet. They shuffle their feet. It dawns on them that they didn't do what was asked. The teacher then calls for attention. She waits until every student is looking at her. She tells them to go back to their seats.

After quickly reviewing her expectations (30 seconds), and without lecturing or raising her voice, she gives her signal for the class to do it again. This time they do it right. She pauses for effect, thanks them for the good day, and sends them on their way.

It comes down to this.

The mistake of course is ever going back on your word. If you say it, if you ask your students of it, then you must back it up with action. Otherwise, your students aren't going to trust you, believe in you, have reason to listen to you, or be inspired by you. What they will do, though, is run right over you.

The first day of school, when you have your students' rapt attention and when their minds are open and they're eager to do well, is the one chance you have to get things right from the beginning.

Whenever your students don't give you what you want, whether it's the first day of school or the last, stop them in their tracks, ask for and wait for their attention, and then make them do it again. Do this whenever they fail to live up to your expectations, and before long, pursuing excellence will become a habit they can't shake.

The Classroom Management Secret

5

A Classroom Management Plan That Works

†

IN HIS BOOK, *Ignore Everybody: And 39 Other Keys To Creativity*, Hugh MacLeod points out that Abraham Lincoln penned the Gettysburg Address on borrowed stationary. Hemingway wrote with a simple fountain pen. Van Gogh rarely used more than six colors on his palate. And MacLeod, himself an artist, sketches cartoons on the back of business cards.

His point is that there is zero correlation between creative talent and the materials and equipment used.

The same can be said about an effective classroom management plan. A simple set of rules and consequences handprinted on ordinary poster board is all you need.

You see, there is no magic in the plan itself. It has no power to influence behavior. Only you have the power to influence behavior by creating a classroom your students want to be part of and then strictly—obsessively—holding them accountable.

Therefore, your plan doesn't need to be elaborate, complex, or involved. It just needs to be followed.

A CLASSROOM MANAGEMENT PLAN IS A CONTRACT

A classroom management plan is a contract you make with your students that promises you will protect their right to learn and enjoy school without interference. Once it's presented to your class, you're bound by this contract to follow it every minute of every day. Otherwise, if you don't, you're breaking your word—and your students' trust.

A classroom management plan has two, and only two, purposes:

1. To state the rules of the classroom.
2. To state exactly what will happen if those rules are broken.

That's it. Some will tell you that you need to include a system of rewards and incentives. But to really change behavior, you have to let go of this idea. The "do this and get that" mentality is a short-term solution that may get you through the day, and thus is a good strategy for substitute teachers, but it won't actually *change* behavior. It won't transform your students into the class you really want.

THE CLASSROOM MANAGEMENT PLAN I RECOMMEND

I recommend the following plan because the rules cover every behavior that could potentially interfere with the learning and enjoyment of your students, and the consequences, when carried out correctly, teach valuable life lessons. It's proven to work regardless of where you teach or who is in your classroom.

Rules:

1. Listen and follow directions.

2. Raise your hand before speaking or leaving your seat.

3. Keep your hands and feet to yourself.

4. Respect your classmates and your teacher.

Consequences:

1st time a rule is broken: Warning

2nd time a rule is broken: Time-Out

3rd time a rule is broken: Letter Home

Be sure and set aside a desk or two for the sole purpose of time-out. The desk doesn't have to be stuck in a corner or far away from the rest of the class. It just must be separated to some degree. It is the symbolic separation from the class and the feelings it evokes that makes time-out effective. It's not a separation of humiliation or gloomy punishment. It's one of reflection, of personal disappointment, and of hope in returning quickly to the class they like being part of.

Create a simple check-off form letter to send home to parents when students reach the third and final consequence. Keep it short and to the point. Refrain from giving your opinion or adding an angry note at the bottom. Just give the facts.

The consequences are in play throughout one single day. When the students arrive for school the next day, lessons have been learned, no grudges are held, and everyone starts fresh—with another chance to succeed, to grow, to be better than the day before.

A Small Role, But A High Priority

A common mistake teachers make is assuming that a classroom management plan is able to do more than its intended and quite narrow purpose. On its own, it provides little motivation for students to behave. Its usefulness comes from how it's implemented, enforced, and carried out, from how you communicate with your students, how much influence you have with them, and how much they enjoy being part of your class.

Your classroom should be exciting and creative. Your classroom management plan, however, shouldn't be. Avoid cutesy and colorful designs. Even kindergarteners need to know that your classroom management plan and the rules by which it governs are sacred, serious. Let it have a look worthy of its utilitarian purpose.

Two large pieces of poster board or construction paper—rules on one, consequences on the other—will do. Put them up on your wall, prominently, so everyone who enters your classroom will know that behaving in a manner that is most conducive to learning is a priority in your classroom. Then honor the contract you made with your students by following it exactly as it's written.

6

Why Coming on Too Strong Will Force a Mutiny in Your Classroom

ọ

WHETHER STARTING OVER from scratch or opening a new school year, many teachers come on too strong when teaching classroom management. Demanding and forewarning, growling and glaring, even the mildest-mannered teachers can become overbearing when it comes to laying down the law in the classroom.

Although most don't consciously or overtly try to scare students into behaving, there is an unmistakable undercurrent of intimidation in the way they present their classroom management plan.

The thinking is that in this day and age you *have* to talk tough. You *have* to carry yourself with a demanding and aggressive presence or your students will walk all over you.

But it isn't true. Fear and intimidation belong in the dark ages of classroom management. The truth is, you can't force today's students into behaving. You can't strong-arm them into listening to you, following your rules, or even caring what you have to say.

You can try, as so many do, but it doesn't work.

Here's why:

The Classroom Management Secret

It creates an us-against-them mentality.

The moment you crossover from being seen as the trusted leader to being viewed as an antagonist or enemy, bad things begin to happen. So by aggressively driving home your classroom management plan, rather than focusing on the teaching and learning of it, you alienate your students before your plan is even in place.

It frames classroom management in a negative light.

When you present behavior expectations with an abrasive, new-sheriff-in-town attitude, it causes students to see classroom management as something negative—as something to object to and rail against. The truth is, effective classroom management is a wonderful and freeing benefit for your students, as well as for you, and you have to present it as such.

It boxes you in.

Coming on too strong will force you to behave similarly whenever you have to deal with misbehavior. Otherwise, your students won't take you seriously. In other words, if you try to enforce a consequence with a calm and pleasant demeanor, for example, but you've already established yourself as a tough-talking disciplinarian, they'll assume you don't really mean it.

It turns you into a mean teacher.

Once you take on the persona of a "mean" teacher, you'll have to carry it with you for the rest of the year—unless you learn a better way. What can be so frustrating to a lot of teachers is that despite being easygoing most of the time, that 5% when dealing with misbehavior marks you as "mean" and unlikable in the eyes of your students.

It makes building rapport and influence a near-impossibility.

I've heard teachers claim that they don't mind if students dislike them. This may be true, but when your students don't like you, your ability to build rapport and influence goes down the drain. And without this ability, you'll always struggle with classroom management. You'll need that "mean" persona and much more just to keep a lid on your classroom.

It encourages rebelliousness.

If your students view your classroom management plan as something that keeps them from enjoying school, rather than the very thing that protects and ensures their right to enjoy school, then they will rebel against it with all their might. It will become something to push against, outsmart, and get away with, causing them to sneak misbehavior behind your back at every turn.

A Better Way

When your focus is on teaching classroom management—through detailed modeling, role-play, and practice—rather than trying to convince students through your tough-as-nails posture that you really mean it, you're free to be yourself, even have fun while presenting your plan.

The good news is that teaching classroom management in this naturally charismatic way is so much more effective, both in the short and long term. Your students will absorb the true purpose of classroom management, seeing it as a necessary but liberating benefit rather than a downpour on their parade.

Whether it's the first day of school or a need to push the restart button on classroom management, it is the first step to creating the class you really want. It is the first step to making your classroom a place your students look forward to coming to every day.

7

How to Teach Your Classroom Management Plan

OF ALL THE RESPONSIBILITIES you have on the first day of school, teaching your classroom management plan is número uno in importance. After all, your success as a teacher hinges on your ability to manage your classroom.

Teachers who are nonchalant about classroom management, or who see it as a nuisance, won't be nearly as effective as those who place it at the top of their list. To put it more plainly, experts in classroom management are better teachers, hands down. They're also happier, more confident, and have healthier relationships with students.

So right out of the gate, after a few opening remarks, you'll do well to dive right in and show your new class exactly what is expected of them by teaching your classroom management plan in a way they'll never forget.

Here's how:

Be Clear.

Bring your classroom management plan into HD focus for your students by making it clear and comprehensible—because ambiguity and confusion are the enemies of effective classroom management. Leave no doubt as to what constitutes following and breaking your rules by shining a light on even the most nuanced misbehavior.

Be Passionate.

It's rarely subject matter that motivates students. It's the teacher and the passion he or she brings to the lesson. Given its importance, teaching classroom management is *the* time to let it out. Allow your students to see the real you, the one determined to create a classroom experience beyond the norm, the everyday, and the colorless, while reaching toward the extraordinary.

Be Dynamic.

Teaching classroom management is a physical experience. To make it real for your students, to make it unforgettable, you must dramatize, model, and perform your way through your plan, vividly showing them what both following rules and breaking them looks and feels like. Walk them through each progressive step a misbehaving student would take.

Be Contrarian.

Use the how-not strategy to demonstrate the most common rule-breaking behaviors students engage in. Sit at a student's desk and show them *how not* to get your attention, *how not* to ask a question, or *how not* to behave during lessons. They must see and experience what isn't okay in order to fully understand what is.

Be Interactive.

Involve your students physically in teaching your plan. Let them role-play scenarios. Allow them to be the teacher while you play the part of a student. Gather them around you, encourage questions, let them take an active role. After all, they have more at stake and more to gain from quality classroom management than even you do.

Be Thorough.

Surprises lead to confusion, resentment, and ultimately more misbehavior. Make sure there is no misunderstanding. Make sure your students know precisely where your boundary lines are. Otherwise, they'll be forever uncomfortable, unsure of themselves, and unable to relax and enjoy the freedom within your boundaries.

Be Skeptical.

For review, ask your students to show you how to ask a question or how to get up to turn in work or how to attend during lessons. Make them prove they understand. Have them demonstrate what following rules does and doesn't look like. If you like, depending on the grade level, you can even devise a written test.

How Often, How Long

One of the most common email questions I get is how long should it take to teach your classroom management plan. An hour or so a day for the first week of school should be enough for initial learning. After that you'll want to review every day for the next three or four weeks. Sometimes this review will only take a few minutes, or as long as it takes to read aloud your plan. Other days you may want to review entire sections in detail.

After three or four weeks, if you've been thorough with your teaching, chances are you'll revisit your plan only occasionally throughout the year. Once per week being a good rule of thumb.

Make It Important

Students are quick to buy into and follow whatever the teacher deems is important. And so when classroom management is shown to be a priority, even if it feels like a complete cultural shift from what they're used to, your students will go right along in agreement. They'll be on board, supporting your desire to make your classroom a special place, bereft of bad attitudes, negativity, rudeness, disruption, and disrespect.

Every student, deep down, when shown the way, wants to do well. They all want to experience the feeling of being more than what they thought they could be. They all want a chance to be a part of something unique and meaningful and remarkable. We all do.

So on that first day, and throughout the first week, when you paint for your students a vigorous and highly detailed picture of what an exceptional classroom looks like . . .

That's exactly what you'll get.

8

How to Be Consistent With Classroom Management

ASK A HUNDRED TEACHERS if it's important to be consistent with classroom management and every last one of them will tell you that it is. But knowing it's important is one thing. Actually being consistent is another.

Most teachers only kinda-sorta follow their classroom management plan, deciding whether to enforce a consequence not based on what their plan actually says, but on the particulars of the situation, how they feel in the moment, or who is doing the rule breaking. But this becomes the slickest of slippery slopes, and before long they're routinely ignoring their classroom management plan.

It's only much later, upon experiencing the extreme stress and upside-down chaos of letting things go, that they kick themselves under their desk and resolve not to let it happen again. But then doubt slowly slithers its way back in, and the cycle repeats.

The solution to classroom management inconsistency isn't intense psychotherapy. It's not Skinnerian conditioning. It isn't even a renewed determination to do better. It's much simpler than that. The solution is confidence, confidence in knowing that it is indeed best to follow through with your classroom management plan every single time.

What follows is a list of reasons why you *must* be consistent with classroom management. Review it often. Internalize its importance. Relax in its reassurance.

And your doubts will be put to rest.

It's unfair not to.

To enforce your agreed-upon consequences sometimes and not others is grossly unfair to your students. *"Why does she get away with calling out in class and I don't?"* Why indeed? And regardless of your reasoning, regardless of the sensitive nature of the circumstances or the unique personality of the misbehaving student, the rest of your class doesn't know any better and thus will be sure to enter it into their unfairness file.

It causes resentment.

If you don't follow your classroom management plan as it's written, the same for every regular education student in your classroom, your students will naturally conclude that you're playing favorites. And they'll fiercely resent you because of it. This can be particularly galling when those few who are given more latitude than others are the same ones who continually disrupt the class and ruin the fun of learning.

You'll lose respect.

Whenever you say you're going to do something and don't do it, you lose a layer of respect from your students. The central message they get from you is that you can't be counted on. You're not a leader they can place their trust in. To them, you're just another wishy-washy adult who makes promise after promise but doesn't come through.

You'll be tested.

When your most challenging students learn that you're not so committed to enforcing consequences, they'll smell blood in the water. Although they'll pick their spots, they'll test you and challenge you every chance they get. They'll continually skirt the edges of your rules, probing for weakness. They'll push the boundaries. They'll hold learning hostage. And they'll drive you crazy.

Behavior will worsen.

Wherever there is weak or semi accountability, behavior, respect, and kindness take a nosedive. That's just the way it is and the way it will always be. Try as we might to bury our heads in the sand and deny it, it's a fact of teaching. We can't get around it. It's the human condition. Of course, the inverse is also true: Where there is accountability, polite behavior, respect, and kindness are sure to follow.

Learning will suffer.

You simply cannot protect the rights of your students to learn and enjoy school if you don't follow your classroom management plan. Calling out in class, getting up without permission, interruptions, side-talking, name-calling, drama, misbehavior, silliness—your students have a right to come to school and learn without interference. And unless you rely on a plan for holding misbehaving students accountable, learning will suffer.

You'll be forever frustrated.

Without 100% reliance on your classroom management plan to curb unwanted behavior, you'll naturally fall into harmful methods like yelling, scolding, sarcasm, arguing, and the like. You'll struggle with anger and emotional control. You'll also find yourself hoping your students will behave, pleading with them to behave, and trying to convince them to behave. This remarkably frustrating and ineffective combination will surely cause you to question your choice of career.

ONE PLAN

There are those who would have you believe that you *should* have different standards of behavior, that you should consider each student and every situation differently and individually and adjust your consequences accordingly.

This may sound good in theory. It may very well play out proudly in academia to enthusiastic applause. But in a real-world classroom it is a disaster. A teacher who dishes out consequences based on his (or her) own, personal subjective view of his students, the behavior in question, or the particular situation will lose control of his classroom and the respect of his students.

A well-written classroom management plan, on the other hand, followed as taught, modeled, and practiced, is fair to all students and never creates resentment, friction, and hard feelings between the teacher and his students.

Unless you have a student in need of specific behavioral accommodations detailed in an Individualized Educational Program (IEP), it's best for your students, their learning, and your peace of mind that they all fall under the same clearly defined, objective classroom management plan.

9

How Best to Inform Students of a Consequence

🔑

HOW YOU GIVE a consequence matters. How you speak to your students, what you say to them, and how you react emotionally and with your body language after they break a classroom rule goes a long way toward curbing misbehavior.

Whether you're giving a warning, a time-out, or a letter to take home, the key is to inform them in a way that takes the focus off of you, and places the responsibility solely with them.

Your students must feel the burden of behaving poorly. Because if they don't, if they don't feel a sense of regret and a greater desire to follow your classroom rules, then your consequences will be ineffective.

What follows are a few guidelines to help you inform your students of a consequence in a way that tugs on their conscience, causes them to reflect on their mistakes, and lets accountability do its good work.

Tell them why.

When a student breaks a classroom rule, tell her (or him) clearly and concisely why she's been given a consequence. Say, "Jenny, you have a warning because you broke rule number two and didn't raise your hand before speaking." Telling them why leaves no room for debate, disagreement, misunderstanding, or anyone to blame but themselves.

Keep your thoughts, opinions, and comments to yourself.

Let the agreed-upon consequence be the only consequence. Refrain from adding a lecture, a scolding, or your two-cents worth. By causing resentment, these methods sabotage accountability. So instead of taking a reflective look at themselves and their misbehavior, your students will grumble under their breath and seethe in anger toward you.

Do not escort to time-out.

If the consequence calls for a time-out, don't escort them there. Getting up and walking to time-out is an important part of the accountability process. It acts as a statement, or an acknowledgement of sorts, that they indeed broke a classroom rule and are ready to take responsibility for it. Also, escorting them can make them *less* motivated to go.

Behave matter-of-factly.

A matter-of-fact tone and body language enables you to hold students accountable without causing friction. Most teachers make a fuss out of misbehavior—reacting angrily, showing disappointment, sighing, rolling eyes. But this can be humiliating for students in front of their classmates, causing them to dislike you and undermining the critical rapport-building relationship.

Be more like a referee, less like a judge.

A referee's job is to enforce rules, not mediate disagreements, which makes being fair, consistent, and composed a lot easier. Thinking like a referee rather than a judge also helps students see that your consequences aren't personal, but something you must do to protect their right to learn and enjoy school.

Safeguard your influence.

An influential relationship with students gives you the leverage you need to change behavior. So anything you do that threatens that relationship—yelling, scolding, lecturing, using sarcasm, etc.—should be avoided. Simply tell your students like it is, follow your classroom management plan, and let accountability do the rest.

Move on.

As soon as you've informed the misbehaving student what rule was broken and the consequence, turn your attention back to whatever you were doing without skipping a beat. The burden of responsibility then shifts in total from you, the mere deliverer of the consequence, to the student. The interaction should take no longer than 10-15 seconds.

Your Students Decide, Not You

Small, seemingly insignificant details, often glossed over, ignored, or deemed too nit-picky to care about, can make a *big* difference. How you inform your students of a consequence is a small part of classroom management, to be sure, a bit player in the theater of your classroom. But it's an important part, requiring an Oscar-level performance.

Despite how much an act of misbehavior may get under your skin or how much you'd like to express your frustrations, you have to stay in character. Because if after receiving a consequence your students blame you, or become angry with you, then the consequence will be ineffective.

They must see that they alone bear the responsibility for their misbehavior. After all, *you* don't decide when or if to enforce a consequence.

Your students do.

10

Why You Should Take Your Time Responding to Misbehavior

⚷

IT'S COMMON PRACTICE for teachers to interrupt misbehavior as it's occurring. The idea being that if you react quickly enough, you'll be able to cut off the wrongdoing before it escalates. This is a typical response from anyone wanting to stay on top of classroom management. And like a beat cop who aggressively tamps down neighborhood trouble before it gets a toehold, it makes sense.

But you're not a police officer, nor should you be so gung-ho to get in on the action. The truth is, becoming involved too quickly is a mistake. It's best to observe from a short distance and respond only after the misbehavior has played itself out.

Here's why:

It allows *you* to be the witness.

If you get involved too soon, it will be a challenge sorting through what happened and who is deserving of a consequence. Confusion is a difficult student's best friend, and by diving in too quickly, you'll be swimming in a sea of denials, arguments, and accusations. Better to let the misbehavior play out and see with your own eyes what happened.

It deescalates the behavior.

By calmly observing misbehavior from a noticeable distance—whereby making students aware of your presence—you keep others from becoming involved, you ensure the safety of all your students, and you eliminate the chance that your early involvement, and the subsequent tension it creates, will cause an escalation in misbehavior.

It saves learning time.

When you allow misbehavior to play out, when you're able to witness what transpires, you save time otherwise spent interviewing students and getting to the bottom of what happened—or what was about to happen. Knowing for certain who is responsible allows you to enforce a quick consequence and be done with it.

It allows for introspection.

A delayed response gives your students a chance to think twice about their misbehavior. In fact, your observing presence all but forces them to make a choice. This window of time provides an opportunity for them to turn from their poor conduct and take responsibility for it. Acknowledging their mistakes without your prompting makes the lesson much more effective.

It keeps you cool.

Interrupting misbehavior is personal, for both you and your students, making it easy to lose your composure, raise your voice, say things you'll regret, and incite anger and pushback from your students. When you observe first, on the other hand, you're able to keep your emotional distance and follow your classroom management plan without causing friction.

WATCHFUL EYES

In taking this more clinical, observant approach to misbehavior, you'll notice a remarkable thing begin to happen. Your students will be less inclined to misbehave. There is something about misbehaving under the direct gaze of a fair and objective teacher that makes students very uncomfortable, like having a video camera recording their every move.

Being observed from a noticeable distance by a teacher committed to following his or her classroom management plan elicits in students a strong, uneasy feeling to turn from their misbehavior and get busy doing what they're supposed to be doing.

As you get better recognizing the early seeds of misbehavior, and getting into position to observe it, your students will grow more and more uncomfortable under the weight of your discerning, watchful eye. They'll know that if they misbehave on your watch, there is no arguing, finger pointing, or clever misdirection. Just consequences.

Following classroom rules, then, becomes a most attractive option.

11

Classroom Management and the Power of Your Personality

ဝ
 l

THE COMMON NOTION that you have to forgo your personality to effectively manage your classroom couldn't be further from the truth. In fact, sharing your uniqueness, your charisma, and your joie de vivre with your students makes classroom management *easier*, not harder.

It's your personality that draws students in, makes you worth listening to, and gives them a compelling reason *to want* to behave. If you're stiff, boring, and spiritless, then no matter how committed you are to following your classroom management plan, you're still going to struggle with misbehavior.

Remember, there is no magic in the plan itself. It's all the other stuff—your likability, rapport, and the learning environment you create—that gives you the leverage to transform your class.

Many teachers, however, find it difficult to tap into that part of themselves that only their closest confidants and family members see. So what follows are a few suggestions to help you step beyond your comfort zone and into a stronger, more influential relationship with your students.

Be yourself.

A classroom is the perfect place to be more you than just about anywhere else. Because of the stark difference in generations, you're free to throw off the social constraints of your age, peers, and professional acquaintances. You can be the real you without the threat of judgment.

Loosen up.

Your students will appreciate any attempt to let your guard down and have some fun for their sake. So loosen up. Tell some stories. Have a laugh together. Never be afraid to show your passion for teaching. For these are the qualities that make building rapport effortless.

Stand tall.

Stooped shoulders, hands on hips, deep sighs. Defeatist behavior constrains your personality and makes you less like the leader your students will want to follow. How you present yourself to your students *matters*. So stand tall, be confident, and resolve to not let anything get under your skin.

Be present.

You don't have to be a martyr who stays late and toils on the weekends for your students. You don't have to be grim-faced and driven, straining for every incremental improvement in behavior. But you do have to be 'on' while with your students. You do have to be awake, alive, and fully present.

Maintain your focus.

Continually remind yourself to enjoy the rewards that come with working with students. Cherish every minute with them—teaching, interacting, inspiring. *This* is your focus.

The meetings, trainings, collaborations, and such? They're just not very important.

Join in.

Joining students in a game or activity they enjoy is a simple way to show off your personality and build easy rapport. So jump in at recess one day for foursquare or soccer, and then notice how differently they look at you and feel about you afterward.

Close the distance.

We talk a lot on the Smart Classroom Management website about not taking misbehavior personally, about how it undermines classroom management. But it also creates distance between you and your students. Your personality, on the other hand, is what draws them closer and endears you to them.

LET IT SHINE

Showing your personality is an easy, natural way to build influence and leverage with your students. So does this mean you have to be silly all the time? Not at all. To a certain degree you still have to pick your moments. But I think most teachers would be amazed at the amount of fun that takes place in well-run, high-achieving classrooms.

Just this morning (I'm writing this on a Tuesday) I walked into a third grade classroom during a math lesson. The teacher was relaxed and cheerful and looked like there was no place in the world she'd rather be. The students were sitting up straight, smiling, and quick to laugh.

I knew walking in that this teacher was one of the best. Her students *love* her, their behavior is superb, and every year they make extraordinary academic progress. And so despite being in the middle of a lesson, we joked and laughed. I told a story. The students were attentive and lovely. It was a pleasure being in their company and experiencing this remarkable teacher's dream class.

So what's her secret? It's simple, really. She is uncompromising with her classroom management plan. Her belief in her students, both behaviorally and academically, is off the charts.

And her personality shines into every corner of the room.

12

Why Laughter Makes Classroom Management More Effective

I HOPE you're reading this. I hope the title piqued your interest. If it did, I'm glad you're here. The topic is a special one. I hope I can do it justice.

Bringing laughter into the classroom is so close to my heart that it makes me apprehensive to write about. I feel like I'm giving away a family secret or that I'm somehow betraying the trust of the hundreds of students I've had over the years and the close bonds we've shared.

You see, laughter is one of the ways I've turned disparate groups of students into my dream class. I know it can do the same for you. For laughter has the ability to soften hardened hearts, open shuttered minds, and endear students to one another.

It is the key that allows a teacher to reach her hand out to the difficult, the unmotivated, the awkward, and the unhappy . . . and have them reach back.

Here are a few more reasons to bring laughter into your classroom:

Your students will love you for it.

When you make an effort to add humor to your lessons, routines, and activities, you instantly become more likable to your students, which causes them to want to be around you, to please you, and to get to know you better. This in turn gives you leverage to influence their behavior.

It's a common language.

Although it can take time for some students to come around, all students like to laugh. Laughter is the one thing guaranteed to build camaraderie and knock down social and emotional walls, binding students from different backgrounds together into one happy classroom.

It's easy.

It takes little or no planning to bring more laughter to your classroom. All you need is a willingness to try. Your students will appreciate any effort to be funny. They're primed to laugh. So be your silly self, tell a joke or two, and show your best—or worst—dance moves.

It builds togetherness.

I'm dubious of community circles, at least in the way they're commonly used. Hashing out grievances can lead to resentment and more things to complain about. Sharing a laugh and having a good time together, however, soothes old wounds and alleviates hurt feelings better than anything else.

It motivates students to behave.

Humor can help you create a classroom your students love being part of. This, along with strict accountability, provides a strong motivator for students to behave. No student wants to wallow in time-out while their classmates are having a laugh with the teacher.

It eases tension.

Many classrooms buzz with tension. You can feel it as soon as you walk through the door. Laughter, however, can relax an uptight classroom—releasing tension, calming vibrating knees, and bringing joy to the room.

It encourages hard work.

When students are happy to be in your class, you can ask so much more of them. They appreciate a classroom they enjoy coming to every day, and they'll want to repay you for it. It's human nature. We reciprocate those we feel indebted to.

It reaches the hard to reach.

Humor has the power to help you make personal connections with students, particularly with those who are hardest to reach. When I look back on the most challenging students I've had over the years, I can often point to the use of humor as a major factor in helping to turn them around and guide them in the right direction.

THE STRAIGHT SCOOP

There is a common belief that if you use humor in your classroom, you'll lose control of your students. But here's the thing: If you already have poor classroom management, then yes, it's true. Trying to be funny will backfire on you, and behavior will likely get worse.

But if you have solid classroom management skills, then bringing more laughter into your classroom will make you even more effective.

And that's the straight scoop.

13

Why Before School is the Perfect Time to Build Rapport

⚷

FIVE MINUTES. That's all it takes to improve your relationship with your students. And why is that important? Because having rapport with students translates to powerful and behavior-influencing leverage—the kind of leverage that compels them to want to behave, to want to do well, and to want to please you.

Those few minutes before the morning bell are perfect for improving relationships and for building a natural, trusting bond between you. But you have to get up from your desk to do it. You have to set aside your lesson plans, walk away from your last minute preparations, and give up your most treasured final moments of morning solitude.

For wherever your students congregate before school—in the hallway, on the playground, lined up outside your classroom—that's where you should be. Chatting, listening, smiling . . . just visiting.

Here's why:

It's an easy way to build rapport.

Simply being with your students outside the limits of the classroom is an easy, organic way to build rapport. But it's important that you bring with you no agenda, no expectations, and no strings attached. Just bring your non-judgmental self and a modest goal of getting to know your students better. They'll take care of the rest.

It's an opportunity to talk with those who talk less.

As your students grow accustomed to your presence every morning, they'll begin drawing closer—sharing personal stories, becoming more familiar, smiling and laughing more, and making eye contact. This is especially important for shy, quieter students. You see, the more comfortable they are with you in these casual moments, the more they'll open up, participate, and contribute in class.

It allows you to prove that every day is a new day.

The idea that yesterday's mistakes and misbehaviors are forgotten is an important part of an overall strategy to turn around your most difficult students. But it doesn't work if they don't believe you or if your actions say otherwise. Thus, spending some quality, no-strings-attached time with them every morning is an especially impactful way to prove this truth to a skeptical bunch.

It brings less popular students into the fold.

No, you're not going to have a particular agenda or awkward strategy to force friendships with less popular students. But what you are going to do is let everyone see who these students really are. You're going to let their personalities blossom and shine. As you build rapport with them, and bring others into the conversation, friendships will develop naturally. You're just a gardener planting seeds.

It's a reminder of what a blessing it is to be a teacher.

The love of teaching can be found in your relationships with students. It's the deep connections, the laughter, the thank yous, the smiles, and the poignant moments you'll always remember—and that can never be taken away. The more time you spend with your students "just because," the more influence you'll have, the better teacher you'll be, and more you'll love your job.

JUST BE YOU

The biggest mistake teachers make when attempting to build rapport is that they try too hard. They dominate the conversation—talking at rather than with students. They shower them with praise. They talk too loud and too aggressively. In other words, they force the relationship and come across as inauthentic.

Having a healthy, trusting, and influential rapport with students, the kind that gives your classroom management plan relevance and meaning, is primarily a function of your likability. So take it easy. Listen more than talk. Don't try so hard. Let the conversation come to you—and then let it go where it goes. Just be there. Be open. Be available.

And most of all, be yourself.

14

Why You Shouldn't Reward Students for Good Behavior

⚷

FOR REGULAR EDUCATION classroom teachers, giving rewards in exchange for good behavior is a mistake.

It's true that "do this and get that" type rewards can improve behavior in the short term. As in, "Sit up straight and give me your attention, and I will give you each a sticker." Or, "John, if you can go the whole day without bothering your tablemates, I have a surprise for you after school."

But incentives of this nature, which include earning class pizza parties, extra recess, free time, and the like, don't benefit students in the long run and make classroom management more difficult. This applies to individual students as well as entire classrooms.

For real, lasting behavior improvement, focus instead on creating a classroom that nurtures intrinsic motivation, and leave the bribery to the trainers at Sea World.

Here's why:

1. Rewards turn good behavior into work.

Rewarding good behavior sends the message to your students that if they have to be paid for it, then it must be work. They logically conclude that being well behaved must be something difficult or noteworthy. Otherwise, why would they be rewarded for it? This effectively makes good behavior less desirable and more like an effort your students deserve to be paid for.

2. Rewards lead to entitlement.

When you offer rewards in return for good behavior, you create in your students a peculiar sense of entitlement. They'll feel entitled to receive something for merely doing what is expected. It leads them to believe that they're behaving and following rules *for you*, and thus are owed something *from you*. After all, if they're getting a reward for it, there must not be anything in it for them.

3. Rewards cheapen the intrinsic motivation to behave.

Being rewarded to behave cheapens the intrinsic merit of being a valued citizen of your class. In other words, it puts a price tag on the priceless. Have you ever had a student who was uncomfortable or less than thrilled with public recognition, drummed up awards, or excessive praise? This is a person with already strong, deep-rooted intrinsic motivation who would prefer that you didn't barter with it.

4. Rewards lead to more and more and more.

When you put a price tag on good behavior by offering rewards, your students will demand higher and more frequent payments. Rewards, you see, are not only ineffective in the long term, but they weaken over time. If you've used rewards in the past, you've experienced this. What is exciting and fun at first, like extra recess, becomes boring and not a big deal after awhile.

Therefore, you have to continue to increase the payment or the frequency of the reward.

The Ultimate Reward

Good behavior is its own reward because it offers students self-respect, confidence, and the wonderful feeling of belonging to a classroom that needs and appreciates them.

To deepen these feelings, and to get your students to *want* to behave—for themselves and for the betterment of your classroom—stop rewarding them for good behavior. Stop interfering with the awesome power of intrinsic motivation.

Instead, support it, encourage it, and feed it by creating a classroom your students love coming to every day. It's the best reward you could ever give them.

15

How Your Classroom Environment Can Improve Behavior

A DISORGANIZED, unkempt, or clutter-filled classroom sends the message to your students that poor behavior and middling work habits are acceptable, regardless of how often or how forcefully you say otherwise. Because if your classroom environment doesn't match your call for excellence, hard work, and respect, then you might as well be talking to the art projects fading and curling on your walls.

Stacked boxes, messy work areas, disorganized and overflowing cabinets, cramped aisles and walkways, papers piled on your desk, various materials and resources jumbled here and there . . . Clearing it all out and replacing it with a clean, organized classroom will do wonders for behavior in your classroom.

Here's why:

It commands reverence.

Adults and students alike walk into bright, neatly arranged classrooms like they're walking into a museum. They sort of tiptoe in, taking great care not to disturb its peacefulness and sacred learning environment.

The Classroom Management Secret

It's inviting.

An attractive classroom draws students in and makes them to want to be part of what is going on inside. All students crave the feeling of being associated with something exclusive, and your classroom environment should communicate to all who enter that indeed it is.

It's a statement of respect.

Your room environment shows how much you value respect—respect for learning, respect for each other, and respect for property. Although they might not be able to verbalize it, your students can see it and feel it every time they walk into your classroom.

It makes you a better, more confident teacher.

A clutter-free classroom will have a powerful effect on you, calming you and sweeping away the mental clutter and discouragement. It's a reminder that you're in control of your classroom and that creating the teaching experience you desire is within your grasp.

It strengthens your influence.

Creating a classroom your students enjoy coming to every day is a key cornerstone of effective classroom management. A fresh, appealing room environment contributes to the feeling that being one of your students is a special experience, which in turn gives you leverage to influence behavior.

It makes a statement.

There are some classrooms you walk into and *know* the teacher expects the best from his or her students. It oozes from the walls and hums through the air, even when empty. In fact, your classroom environment is an uncanny predictor of how effective a teacher you are.

It gives students a sense of pride.

Students notice everything—from the way you dress to how you speak to what your desk looks like. If you take pride in your classroom and how you go about your job, then your students will follow your lead, taking pride in themselves, their behavior, and their schoolwork.

It calms and focuses.

Some classrooms look like they've been tipped upside down and shaken. In 100% of the cases, students in such classrooms are unhappy, unruly, and climbing the walls. A sharp-dressed classroom, on the other hand—full of pride, respect, open walkways and clear desktops—is a calming, safe-haven to students, allowing them to breathe easy and focus on learning.

EXCELLENCE IS EXPECTED

Your classroom environment has such a strong bearing on how your students perceive themselves and the expectations you have for them that you can't afford to let it fall into disarray or get swallowed up by accumulated materials or cluttered hodgepodge.

Armed with a free weekend and a little perspiration, you can send a powerful and unmistakable message to your students, one that whispers to them every time they walk into your classroom . . .

"Excellence is expected."

16

A Classroom Management Secret Top Teachers Use

♀

AN EARLY MENTOR for me was a teacher named Chuck. Chuck taught sixth grade and was a master at classroom management. In him I was able to see what was possible. I can remember how impressed I was when two or three days into my teaching career I saw him leading his students across campus.

All 36 of them were walking in two perfect lines as Chuck followed from a distance of about 30 feet. They were calm and focused and walked with a casual purpose, displaying a level of maturity I had not seen before.

The two lines would not, however, be characterized as militaristic. And I would soon learn that Chuck was far from the dictator type—quite the opposite. He was kindly and gentle and, although firm and exacting, never raised his voice.

Shortly after, I approached my principal and asked her if I could observe Chuck while he was teaching a lesson. She made arrangements for someone to cover my class for an hour or so, and within a few days I was on my way over to his room.

As I walked up the ramp leading into his portable classroom, I peered through a front window and noticed his students working in groups. They were wrapping heavily salted chicken legs in gauze to simulate an ancient Egyptian mummification process.

As I reached for the door, little did I know that I was in for a surprise other adults on campus had grown accustomed to.

When I stepped inside the room, the student nearest me quickly got to his feet as he nudged the student next to him on the arm. His group in turn immediately dropped what they were doing, stood, and faced me. The rest of the groups followed suit, and within two or three seconds every student in the room was silent, standing, and facing me.

Having the relaxed look of one who *knows* his students will behave as expected, Chuck smiled and greeted me. We exchanged a few words while his students remained attentive. Chuck then introduced me, thanked his students for being respectful, and released them to continue their work.

For the rest of the hour I wandered about his room, talked to students, and watched as Chuck periodically asked for attention to give more instructions. His students were engaging, friendly, and unfailingly polite. It was clear they had great respect and admiration for their teacher.

I was impressed and fortunate to see for myself, just days into my career, that excuses for poor behavior—from teachers, parents and the students themselves—are just that, excuses. Chuck proved to me what was possible at a school that had a reputation for being an especially challenging place to teach.

But despite his exceptional work, not everyone on campus was so impressed with Chuck's attention to detail or his highly specific expectations for basic procedures like walking in line or how to react when an adult walks into the room.

I began hearing grumbling from other teachers and noticing eye rolls whenever anyone brought up Chuck's class. They couldn't understand why such seemingly petty things mattered so much to him. They found his penchant for explicitly teaching the finer points of walking from point A to point B unnecessary, even silly.

But these eye rollers just didn't get it, which is one reason why they spent so much learning time reminding, demanding, and pleading with their students.

You see, Chuck understood a secret to effective classroom management that so many others fail to grasp. The way your line looks when you walk across campus and the way in which your students give their attention when you ask for it, as well as a few other indicators, are measures of your classroom management effectiveness.

Watching a teacher lead his or her students across campus tells you a lot about that teacher and the amount of learning taking place in the classroom. The reason is simple: How students handle everyday routines, like walking in line, reveals how they handle more important matters like, for example, working together in groups.

A line of students can indicate:

- How much they respect their teacher.
- How much they respect each other.
- How well they follow directions.
- How ready they are to receive instruction.
- The amount of time spent on—or off—task in the classroom.

The Classroom Management Secret

Now, I know some teachers claim that they only focus on what they feel is most important, that although their line may not be great while walking across campus, they assuredly expect attentiveness and respect in the classroom.

But this argument doesn't hold water. Having different behavior expectations based on the importance of an activity doesn't work because it sends a confusing message to students. Further, it sets a bad precedent, provides a bad example, and creates bad habits, especially for and among those students who have a proclivity for poor behavior.

On the other hand, clear expectations and explicit guidance on how to perform basic routines and procedures like walking in line will translate to and be compatible with those learning skills that must take place in the classroom. In effect, a line is a perfect learning lab, where students can practice the skills needed to be successful in the classroom—and without the loss of class time.

So next time you get a chance, put your class to the test. Send them off in a line as you follow from behind. Watch closely because it accurately measures your classroom management effectiveness and, consequently, your effectiveness as a teacher.

17

How to Teach Routines

ǫ

ANYTHING YOU ASK your students to do repeatedly should be made into a routine. For example, whenever your students enter your classroom, transition from one activity to the next, or line up for recess, they should do so in the same efficient manner.

The reason, simply put, is that routines save learning time. They also make your life a lot easier.

You see, it's during these repeatable moments when most misbehavior occurs. The idea then is to standardize these moments into routines your students can do quickly and independently.

But here's the thing: Most teachers don't teach routines very well, and the timesaving value gets lost in the stress of reminding, reteaching, and repeating yourself over and over again.

The key is to teach routines in a way that compels your students to perform them correctly, and without your input, every single time.

Here's how:

1. Model how to.

Start your lesson seated at a student's desk—or wherever the routine is to begin—and simply *show* your class what you want them to do. Make it simple and straightforward, but highly detailed. Play the part of a student and act out each step, down to the smallest detail.

2. Model how not.

Call upon your experience in the past and model *how not* to perform the routine. It's okay to have fun with it. In fact, exaggerating poor behavior makes the strategy more effective because it underscores the absurdity of misbehaving in your peaceful classroom.

3. Have a student model.

Now choose one student to perform the routine from start to finish. If you see even the smallest mistake, the smallest deviation from the script, have the student go back and do it again. Ask for a few more volunteers, and again, hold each one to the highest standard.

4. Have a group model.

Select four or five students to model the routine as a group. Observe carefully and continue to be exacting in your expectations, even if it feels like you're overdoing it. (You're not.) The smallest, most insignificant details are what resonate with students the most.

5. Practice with the whole class.

Now ask your entire class to perform the routine together. Have them practice until they get it right. Once they've proven they can do it without any guidance, be sure to let them know. Your students must experience what success feels like in order to repeat it.

6. Go live.

As soon as you're able, have your students perform the routine as a regular part of the school day. Again, you want them to get used to the feeling of success, of doing things the right way. If it's not perfect, then send them back where they started and have them do it again.

Note: Perfection does not mean robotic or militaristic. It simply means performing the routines as taught. You can make them as casual or informal as you wish.

PURSUERS OF EXCELLENCE

Routines save time, dissuade misbehavior, and make your teaching life a lot easier, to be sure. But their real power comes from their ability to transfer excellence to everything you do.

Pushing in chairs, lining up for lunch, behaving politely, dividing fractions—it's all the same steady drip, drip, drip of excellence you require of your students. It's your calm insistence on doing things the right way, starting from the first day of school and cross-pollinating from one routine and one subject area to another . . .

Until it clicks, and your class of disparate individuals becomes a class of students, of scholars, of pursuers of excellence.

The Classroom Management Secret

18

Why You Need to Draw a Line in the Sand With Difficult Students

 x

THERE ARE STUDENTS who have learned from an early age that if they misbehave enough, if they disrupt, interfere, and otherwise make life miserable for everyone around them, then they can get the adults in their life to give in and give them what they want. They develop and refine their technique at home first, then bring it with them to school.

In response most teachers try to hold them accountable—in the beginning anyway. They lecture and admonish. They take away recess. They call home. But this particular brand of difficult student isn't so easily deterred. For he (or she) knows from experience that if he ratchets up his misbehavior, making it more frequent or more outrageous, the teacher will begin treating him differently.

You see, in an effort to shield the other students, as well as herself, from such craziness and disruption, she (the teacher) will begin walking on eggshells around him and ignoring his less disruptive behaviors, which is the first step down a slippery slope.

Before long she'll be offering praise, prizes, and special privileges for *not* disrupting the class—playing into his hands. The student in turn will see himself as special, as though the normal rules of society don't apply. He'll brazenly leave his seat and wander the room when he feels like it. He'll side-talk when the teacher talks. He'll do what he pleases, following directions only when it suits him.

All because he's got his teacher over a barrel. All because his teacher would rather make a deal with the devil than endure one of his temper tantrums. All because she knows his behavior could get worse, perhaps much worse, if she doesn't play his humiliating game.

But it doesn't have to be this way.

The Alternative

One of the traits that separate great teachers and classroom managers from the rest is that somewhere along the line they've decided not to participate in this game. They've decided that the integrity of their classroom will not be purchased for any price.

An Orangutan escapee from the Bronx Zoo could show up on their roster, but she (or he) would have to follow the same rules as everyone else. She may be swinging from the ceiling lights and long-calling at the top of her lungs, but until she does her time-out and proves she can live up the teacher's standards, she won't participate as a regular member of the class.

And here's the interesting thing, the salient point. Teachers who take this stand, those who decide that *nothing* and no one will cause them to relax their behavior standards—which they know are best for their students—are rewarded for it.

You see, when a teacher makes this stand, which is nothing more than a personal, internal decision, somehow, some way, the students know. They just know. Maybe it's the empowerment the teacher carries with her like talisman. Maybe it's her presence or charisma or leadership that fills every room she enters. Maybe it's her vibe sending out a clear communiqué to every student that there are no negotiations, no arguments, and no games-playing. The rules are the rules. That's just the way it is.

When your students know that you'll never participate in unspoken deals, bribes, or quid pro quos, then almost magically their behavior changes.

Now when you first make this decision—or whenever you have a new class or a new group of students—you may still be tested. You may still get a fit of anger, a loud outburst, a brazen challenge. Despite your new vibe and solemn promise to follow your classroom management plan as it's written, there are students whose bristly reactions to being told they can't do whatever they want are so ingrained that they'll put you to the test.

They'll leave their seats and pester other students. They'll yell and pound their desk if you don't put them in the group they want. They'll hum or sing or cry while in time-out. But if you stick to your guns and hold them accountable for every act of misbehavior, it will stop.

The bottom line is that when you draw a line in the sand and decide that nothing on earth will get you to move it, every student within the four walls of your classroom will be changed because of it.

THE FLIP SIDE

Alas, there is a flip side. Most teachers haven't drawn this line—and never will. Although they may have a classroom management plan, although they may have specific rules and defined consequences, they are in fact open to manipulation and deal making. And somehow, someway, the students know.

They know that a tantrum or a dramatic stomping out of the classroom early in the year will soften the teacher up and pay dividends the rest of the way. They know that henceforth the mere threat of a tantrum will afford them special privileges. They know they can get a little breathing room because they have in their back pocket the ability to spoil a lesson, disrupt an afternoon, or ruin the teacher's day.

So they get up from their seat when the mood strikes. They tap their pencil and sigh loudly through your most inspiring lessons. They talk to their neighbors instead of doing their work. They do it because they can. They do it because they know you'll look the other way in the face of these relatively minor misbehaviors. They do it because of the unspoken deal between you.

And although you may warn, remind, and pull them aside for a talking-to, they know that these are nothing more than suggestions. It's a disheartening, powerless way to teach.

Sing A New Song

The only way off this tilt-o-world ride is to begin singing a new song. The only way to end the wink-wink dealmaking in your classroom, and transform your most difficult students into valued, productive citizens, is to pull the trump card out of your back pocket.

There is nothing to fear. There is nothing to lose. Go ahead. Pull out the card. Now lean over, reach down, and draw a line in the sand.

19

Why You Shouldn't Ask Misbehaving Students to Explain Themselves

⚷

WHEN INDIVIDUAL STUDENTS misbehave, it's common practice for teachers to pull them aside and ask why they did what they did. But rarely is it a simple request—because the majority of students will be less than forthcoming in their response. They'll deny and distract. They'll argue and blame others. They'll dig in their heels. Seldom will they provide a satisfactory answer.

Teachers, understandably frustrated, will then demand an explanation. They'll glare and jib-jab their finger. They'll apply pressure. They'll box-in and question like a lawyer sparring with an uncooperative witness. And regardless of how the standoff ends, both parties will walk away annoyed with the other and feeling as if they lost something in the skirmish.

Although it is among the most commonly used methods of classroom management, pulling students aside to explain their misbehavior is a mistake.

Here's why:

It's hard to put into words.

Most students have a difficult time articulating why they misbehaved, especially because they know you won't like the answer. *"Because I felt like it"* sounds disrespectful and is likely to further raise your ire. But it's true, when students misbehave it's because, in that particular moment, they felt like it.

It causes resentment.

With no acceptable answer to give, students feel cornered and either clam up, argue, or lie about what happened, which makes the teacher more determined than ever to browbeat an answer from them.

This unnecessarily brings resentment and distrust into a relationship that must be positive and trusting if you're to influence their behavior for the better.

The teacher's motives are mixed up.

Most teachers don't really want or need to know why students misbehave. They ask because they want them to accept responsibility. They want them to "face the music" and be held accountable for their actions. But this is what a classroom management plan is for—to hold students accountable for every act of misbehavior.

The difference is that a classroom management plan isn't personal and doesn't cause friction in the relationship.

It undermines real, effective accountability.

To students on the receiving end of a teacher interrogation, those several minutes feel like a consequence, especially if it ends with a lecture or a *"Do you understand me?"* So when you add a time-out or a loss of recess to the equation, they feel so bitter that the last thing they're going to do is reflect on their mistake. Instead, because you made it personal, they'll blame you, which is no accountability at all.

It's stressful.

Pulling students aside in an attempt to convince, persuade, manipulate, or use your words to personally hold them accountable is one of the greatest causes of teacher stress. And because it offers only a temporary cessation of unruly behavior, and not true and lasting change, it's a management style you'll have to use every day—or even every hour. Ouch!

It's Your Relationships

For classroom management to be most effective, your students must view your consequences as something they bring deservedly upon themselves, and for which they're solely responsible.

This isn't possible when you make it personal. It isn't possible when you force an explanation for something you already know the answer to. It isn't possible when you go back on your word by circumventing your classroom management plan.

Certainly you can be disappointed with students who misbehave, and in the right moment, you should tell them so. But lecturing individual students and demanding why they did this and that is a mistake that will backfire on you every time.

You can't afford to weaken the bonds you make with your students—or obliterate them altogether with one ugly confrontation. It's your likability and rapport and the one-on-one connections you make, after all, that give you the leverage you need to change behavior.

20

What to Do When a Student Refuses to Go to Time-Out

♀

WHEN A STUDENT REFUSES to go to time-out, he (or she) often has a good reason. This doesn't mean he isn't responsible for making such a decision. He is, completely and fully. For it's never okay to defy a teacher's direction.

But in his mind he feels like he must take a stand. In other words, there is something about the situation or incident that doesn't sit right with him. Asking him to go to time-out, then, crosses the line of his brand of fairness.

So before answering *what* to do, it's important we unpack *why* a student would refuse to go to time-out. Because if a student feels strongly enough to challenge a teacher's directive, then it's a red flag that there are deeper problems in need of addressing.

Difficult students in particular have an acute sense of fairness. So if the way you manage your classroom is unfair, or perceived to be unfair, then it isn't at all unusual to experience at times aggressive pushback. In fact, defiant behavior would be expected in such a classroom.

What follows are four reasons why a student would refuse to go to time-out. Clean these up first. Get them fixed and squared away. And then, although a refusal to go to time-out could still happen, it would be as rare as a class set of encyclopedias.

1. Your students don't understand your classroom management plan.

If a student breaks a classroom rule, but doesn't believe she (or he) did anything wrong, then there is a good chance she'll become defiant. This is one of many reasons why it's so important to teach, model, role-play, and practice your classroom management plan thoroughly.

Your students need to know and experience your plan backwards and forwards—why it's important, why it's wrong to break rules, and exactly step-by-step what will happen if they do. There should never be any surprises, disagreements, or misunderstandings.

Just it-is-what-it-is accountability.

2. You're inconsistent.

If ever you let misbehavior go without a consequence, you're asking for trouble. Your most difficult students will grow especially bitter if you look the other way when another student breaks a rule—because they know they're rarely afforded such luxury.

So when you send them to time-out, it's only natural to get resistance. Teachers who have their rules and consequences on a sliding scale, open to their whims, biases, and interpretations, struggle mightily with classroom management—because it's unfair, and students know it.

3. There is friction between you and your students.

Students resent teachers who yell, scold, lecture, and otherwise take misbehavior personally. It makes them feel like they're being picked on and singled-out, which causes them to fight back by increasing their disruptive activities, particularly behind the teacher's back.

Worse yet, because the teacher doesn't let the agreed-upon consequences be the only consequences (i.e., adding sarcasm, lectures, sighs, eye-rolls, etc.), the students begin to view their teacher as spiteful, unfair, and unlikable.

4. There are uncertainties surrounding the incident of misbehavior.

Before sending a student to time-out, it's important to be sure a rule has been broken. If you're not positive, if you didn't personally witness the incident, then it's best to investigate until you know the truth. Getting it wrong can cause students to shut down, lash out, or sever their trust and belief in you.

By the same token, it's important to be clear with students why you're sending them to time-out. Tell them plainly what rule was broken and what the consequence will be. When caught red-handed and confronted directly, few students will disagree or make a fuss.

NOW, WHAT TO DO

If, after eliminating the reasons above, the improbable happens and a student refuses to go to time-out, then handling it is easy. Say, "Before you make that choice I'm going to give you two minutes to think about it. If after two minutes, you're still sitting here, then I'm going to prepare a letter for you to take home to your parents." (The third consequence.)

Then turn and go back to whatever you were doing. It's now out of your hands and completely the student's decision. As far as you're concerned, because you've eliminated any valid reason why he (or she) would refuse to go to time-out, what he decides doesn't affect you in the least.

It's his choice. And when a student knows it's his choice, and that he's not going to get any coaxing or prodding from you, or get even the slightest rise out of you, then it's a near certainty he's going to quietly stand and take himself to time-out.

And if he doesn't? Que será, será. Follow your classroom management plan. Do what you promised you'd do. After he cools down—perhaps even forgotten about the incident—approach casually, hand him his letter, and say, "I want this signed and returned in morning."

And then get on with your day.

21

How to Talk to Difficult Students

♀

MOST TEACHERS TALK to difficult students too much—because somewhere along the line they've gotten the idea that the more attention they give them, the more effective they'll be. So they pull them aside for pep-talks, reminders, and lectures. They warn. They scold. They threaten. They flatter and praise. They argue and manipulate.

They spend more time addressing them, conferencing with them, and trying to persuade them to behave than the rest of their class put together. And for the most part, it's a waste of time.

This doesn't mean that talking with difficult students can't have a positive effect. When done in a certain way, and in the right moment, it most definitely can.

Here's how:

Make it infrequent.

Difficult students have been on the receiving end of near-constant talking-tos for as long as they've been in school. When they see you coming with that same familiar look on your face, they roll their eyes. They've heard it all. To get them to see themselves as capable of following rules like anyone else, you shouldn't touch base with them more than anyone else.

The Classroom Management Secret

Make it honest.

In a desperate attempt to improve behavior, many teachers will say just about anything to difficult students, regardless of its truthfulness. But trying to coerce students into behaving, particularly while being less than honest, doesn't work. Neither does false praise, bribing, or any other form of manipulation. The most effective way to talk to difficult students is to give it to them straight.

Make it meaningful.

The only reason to talk to difficult students about their behavior is to inform or to deepen the meaning of a lesson *already learned*. Never ask them why they did this or that. Never force assurances or explanations. Never give them a dressing-down. Let their mistakes and subsequent accountability, or their successes and subsequent good feelings, be the lesson. Don't ruin it, absolve it, or weaken it with your overinvolvment.

Make it a challenge.

When difficult students misbehave, let your classroom management plan do your talking for you. However, if the right moment strikes, and you know a word or two can provide additional strength and meaning to the lesson, then make it an encouraging challenge. For example, you might cruise by their desk or time-out chair and say simply, *"You're better than that."*

Make it wordless.

When a difficult student does something well or has a particularly good day, it's often best not to say anything at all, which is a startling change when compared to most of his or her former teachers (who'd all but throw a parade). By simply not making a big deal out of them doing what they're supposed to do, what they're expected to do, you send a powerful, behavior-altering message.

Make it a gesture.

If a difficult student has several good days, or you're convinced he or she has made real improvement, and not just a brief period of acceptable behavior, then a simple gesture like a fist bump or a knowing smile can be especially impactful. It can deepen the meaning of a positive lesson already learned. And unlike silly, over-the-top celebrations for moderate improvement, the student's heart will soar—internally, privately, and resoundingly.

Make it free of strings.

Most teachers only talk to difficult students when they want something from them (i.e., improved behavior), which effectively poisons the relationship. To influence their behavior you have to build mutual, trusting rapport, which only comes with no strings attached. Decide to like and enjoy your most difficult students so that when you do talk to them about their behavior, what you say will pack a punch.

Let Them Stand...

Teachers spend so much time and attention on difficult students because it makes them feel like they're doing *something* to help improve their behavior. They figure that if they work hard enough on the problem, if they can just somehow come up with the right words to say, they'll be able to turn them around.

But the more attention you give to difficult students, the less attention they'll pay to what you say and the harder it will be to improve their behavior. So instead of telling them how they should feel, what they should think, and what lessons they should be learning, give them a chance to feel the weight of their mistakes and the inner joy of their successes. Let them stand on their own two feet.

Then, and only then, will the wellspring of change come bubbling up from the only place it truly can:

From within.

22

6 Powerful, Soul-Searching Things You Can Say to Difficult Students

♀

WHEN IT WAS FIRST PUBLISHED online, we had a large email response to the previous chapter. Most readers wrote to express how much easier dealing with difficult students had become after putting the suggestions to use. But others wanted specifics. They wanted to know exactly *what* to say to difficult students—and when.

Excellent questions, to be sure, and I was thrilled to revisit one of my favorite topics. But before moving ahead, it's important to note that unless you hold your most challenging students accountable, then little of what you say will make a difference—because the words you use only hold meaning for them inasmuch as they deepen, underscore, or highlight lessons already learned. A timely word or two, though, can help bring these sometimes-hard lessons to life, allowing students to see their mistakes—and successes—in a new light.

The right words can also help build rapport and influence, buoy sagging spirits, and provide that metaphorical kick in the pants all of us need once in a while. Below you'll find six powerful, soul-searching phrases, none of which require an outward response from students. In fact, they're more effective if you don't wait for one. For these are words you leave with them—

to ponder, marinate in, and grapple with—not words that require anything from them.

And like the flash and crack of unexpected lightening, they're sure to get their attention.

1. *"You're better than that."*

When: After an incident of misbehavior, perhaps while the student is sitting in time-out.

Why: It is both a statement of fact and a challenge, and coming from someone they respect, four little words never said so much. Like flipping a switch, it's a remark that can instantly change a student's attitude from feeling sorry for himself (or herself) or proudly smug to determined not to make the same mistake again.

2. *"This is not who you are."*

When: At the end of a bad day, perhaps while the student is reading the behavior letter you presented him or her to take home.

Why: Through their words and actions, most teachers communicate to difficult students that their misbehavior *is* who they are, all but guaranteeing that poor behavior will not only continue, but get worse. This comment, though, said with calm conviction, assures them that it isn't true.

3. *"That's not good enough."*

When: After a period of improvement.

Why: Difficult students are used to receiving heavy praise for modest improvement, and so this statement can come as a shock. At first glance it appears to be a criticism, but in effect it's a powerful morale booster—because it lets them know that you believe in them, and that they're capable of so much more.

4. *"You can do this."*

When: Before trusting them with a delicate task or assignment, one that in the past would have tripped them up and caused unwanted behavior.

Why: As you begin to see improvement, you *must* give difficult students opportunities to take the next step. And so just before sending them off to work on a class project with their friends, for example, look them in the eye and make this remark with fist-pumping intensity.

5. *"Now that is how you do it!"*

When: After real success—not just improvement, mind you, and not simply a brief moment in time, but a clear and convincing change in behavior.

Why: From behavior contracts to scoldings to meaningless praise, most difficult students have been told they're different for so long that failure becomes part of their DNA. This statement tells them otherwise, assuring them that they don't have to be any better or try any harder. It's living, breathing proof that they really can do it.

6. *"I believe in you."*

When: After hitting rock bottom.

Why: When a difficult student is feeling down about his (or her) misbehavior, it's best to leave him alone with his thoughts. So many teachers interrupt this essential self-examination by trying to soften the blow, which spoils the lesson. After giving him time and space, however, this passing remark can mean the world to him.

LIKE AN ANGEL

Because they've known so many of them, because they've been manipulated, coddled, indulged, and falsely praised ten times over, difficult students can pick a phony a mile away. So unless you genuinely believe in what you're saying, it's best not to say anything at all.

But sparingly used and in the right moments, with just the right tone and intonation, and with stripped down, unadulterated, eyeball-to-eyeball honesty, your words can have power.

And so when you appear unexpected, like a guardian angel from on high, and deliver the message they most need to hear, it will echo in their head long after you've turned and walked away.

23

A Simple Way to Build Rapport With Difficult Students

DIFFICULT STUDENTS behave the way they do because somewhere along the line the ball was dropped. Standards were lowered. Rules were ignored. Excuses were made. Relationships were broken—or were never developed to begin with.

But fate has intervened, and it has been left to you to pick up the ball. Indeed, you are the right person, at the right time, and in the right place.

To start you'll want to hold them to the same rules, standards, and expectations as everybody else, no exceptions. You must decide that no matter what, you'll be remembered for this. *"Mrs. Jones never let me slide. She always believed in me."*

The next step is to begin building rapport, though gently at first, for building rapport is about trust. It's about truth and honesty and making a connection that has the power to change behavior. It can't be rushed, forced, or wrestled to the ground like an opponent. Coming on too strong is a common mistake. *"Hey Anthony! What's up, dude! Got your backpack all zipped up, lookin' good? Awesome! Put'er there, mojambo!"*

No, with difficult students it pays to be more subtle. Remember, these are students who've heard it all and been subjected to every shortsighted strategy under the sun—from fire-breathing admonishments to flat out bribery. Understandably, they're guarded and skeptical of too-forward, too-familiar adults.

To reach them, you must go in through the side door. One of the most effective ways to do this is with a simple note, written in your hand, folded over, and taped to the top or side of their desk. You can leave it while they're at recess or lunch, or after they leave for the day.

What you say in your note is less important than its genuineness. For if you don't truly believe what you say, your students will find you out.

The idea is to begin building a relationship organically—one based on trust and likability. False praise and manipulation will backfire every time. So keep it simple, brief, and understated, and make sure it reflects how you really feel.

I believe in you, Anthony, and I'm proud to have you as a member of this classroom. -Mrs. Ricks

You mustn't mention the note to the student and it's best not to watch them while they read it. Allow them their moment of privacy, while you move on with your day. Chances are they will approach you to say thank you, but not always.

If they do, say simply, "I meant what I said. I thought you should know." There is no need to make any more of it than that.

You won't use these notes every day or even every week. You'll use them once or twice during the first couple of weeks and then only when it feels right. Fortunately, effective classroom management isn't a robotic series of steps. The nuances of teaching—the relationships, the shared moments, the private victories—are where you'll find the greatest pleasure and meaning.

An oft-repeated phrase on the Smart Classroom Management website is that there is no magic to your classroom management plan. Your rules and consequences, although critically important, in and of themselves don't have the power to change behavior.

The magic is in your relationship with your students. And these little notes, appearing out of nowhere, raining down like pixie dust on the unexpected, spread your influence beyond the well-behaved, the self-assured, and the aiming-to-please and into the hearts of your most challenging students. They break down barriers, they draw students in, and they connect you in ways that face-to-face interactions cannot.

Many difficult students have such an unfavorable view of teachers that simply approaching them causes their defenses to go up. Because of their bad relationships with teachers in the past, they see them as all alike. This is why they can be so disrespectful before even getting to know you.

A simple note, though, just between the two of you, has a way of cutting through their negative view of school and of teachers. It cuts through the layers of bad blood, private hurts, and distrust—and touches a soft spot. A place they can't ignore. A place that opens a line of rapport that has the power to change behavior.

24

How to Avoid Labeling Difficult Students

¡

HOPING TO HEAD OFF misbehavior before it starts, most teachers try to be proactive with difficult students. Even before the bell rings on the first day of school, they peruse their new roster looking for those few whose reputation precedes them.

They chat up previous teachers. They scrutinize student files. They nervously begin conjuring up creative ways of dealing with them, all before they even set foot in the classroom.

So when Anthony or Karla or whoever shows up for the first day of school, they can feel the bull's-eye on their back. They can sense the proximity, the attention, and the intensity from their new teacher. They can feel labeled right out of the gate.

And when students feel labeled, they're pulled inexorably in its direction, fulfilling the prophecy it foretells. To ensure this doesn't happen on your watch, and to get your reputed difficult students headed in the right direction, it's best to make them feel like just another member of your classroom.

Here's how:

1. Don't seat them closest to you.

When a student with a difficult reputation walks in on the first day and is asked to sit closest to the teacher, she (or he) knows the score. She knows instantly that she won't be able to leave the mistakes and failures of the previous year behind her. She thinks, *"Here we go again, so I might as well give the teacher what he expects."*

2. Don't spend more time with them.

Kids are smarter than most adults give them credit for. Sure, some may be two grade levels behind in reading, but they'll pick up on nuances in your behavior like a primatologist. Your extra attention and frequent check-ins communicate loud and clear that you've got your eye on them, creating a distrustful relationship right from the get-go.

3. Don't speak to them any differently.

It's common for teachers to speak to difficult students differently than others, without even realizing it. They smile and gab with some as if they don't have a care in the world, but in the next instant their face goes blank and their voice drops three octaves when they turn to speak to Anthony or Karla. It's like saying, *"I don't want you in my class, I don't believe in you, and I expect you to misbehave."*

4. Don't bring up the previous year.

By way of warning, it's a common tactic to let difficult students know in no uncertain terms that you're aware of their previous behavior problems. But this undermines your ability to build rapport. It puts you at odds and in competition and makes them want to push your buttons, get under your skin, and misbehave behind your back.

5. Don't ignore their misbehavior.

Another common strategy, particularly in the beginning of the year, is to ignore less serious, less disruptive behavior from difficult students. But this is yet another obvious sign to them that they're not like everybody else. Misbehavior, silliness, and distraction then become their identity rather than something they can control.

ONE STANDARD

When you treat difficult students differently than their classmates, when you employ strategies, tactics, and teacher behaviors meant only for them, in effect you're telling them that they're incapable of behaving like a successful student. It reinforces the message that misbehaving is who they are, like their eye color or shoe size, boxing them in and weighing them down by the label draped over their shoulders like a wet winter coat.

And when it happens the first week of school, when you make it clear that you've got your eye on them, you're setting them up for failure. You're setting them up for yet another frustrating, here-we-go-again school year. They become the clown prince or princess of your classroom, sadly feigning to take nothing seriously and having no care for tomorrow.

Lasting change happens when we show students, when we prove to them, through our actions and our commitment to the same soaring standards as everyone else . . . that we believe in them.

25

How to Respond to a Disrespectful Student

⚷

WHEN CONFRONTED with disrespect, it's easy to take it personally. This is a normal reaction from a passionate teacher. But it's a colossal mistake, because when you take misbehavior personally, you're likely to react in ways that make managing that student much more difficult. Your leverage and influence will then plummet right along with his (or her) behavior.

If, however, you can refrain from doing what comes naturally, then you can hold the disrespectful student accountable and still retain your ability to influence future behavior.

Here's how:

Lose the battle.

When a student is disrespectful to you, you have to be willing to lose the battle. In other words, you must resist the urge to admonish, scold, lecture, get even, or otherwise attempt to put the student in his place.

Let it go.

Disrespect comes from a place inside the student that has nothing to do with you. So let it go, and don't take it personally. Your job is to help the student see the error of his ways so that it doesn't happen again.

Stay calm.

Take a deep breath to quell any angry feelings rising up inside you. Remind yourself that you'll be much more effective, and the situation will go much smoother, if you maintain emotional control.

Pause.

In the immediate moments following the incident, don't say a word. Simply maintain eye contact with the student and wait. Let his words hang in the air for several seconds, leaving no doubt about what was said, how it was said, and who is responsible for saying it.

End it.

It's important not to escalate the situation, but to end it as quickly as possible. Your pause and unwillingness to react is unnerving and will leave the student devoid of anything to say. As soon as you break eye contact and walk away, the incident is over.

Move on.

Refrain from enforcing a consequence—for now. Just continue on with whatever you were doing. Leave the student standing there, unsure of what to do. It's always best to get back to normalcy as quickly as possible for the sake of the rest of your class.

Do nothing.

Proceed with your day as if nothing happened. Don't approach the student. Don't try to talk to him about what happened. Don't do anything until you're confident that the student has mentally moved on from the situation.

Enforce.

As soon as the student is calm and the incident is forgotten, approach and deliver your consequence. I recommend bypassing the warning step of your classroom management plan and sending the student directly to time-out. Say simply, "You broke rule number four. Grab your work and go to time-out."

Notify.

For overt disrespect, parents should be notified. A letter home is most effective. It also adds a layer of accountability that lasts beyond the day of the incident. Near the end of the school day, hand the student your letter and walk away—without adding a lecture. Let accountability speak for you.

Let remorse set in.

When you handle disrespect this way, without lecturing or scolding or taking it personally, even the most obstinate student will be affected by his mistake. So much so that you're likely to get a sincere and unforced apology.

A Lesson Learned

By following these steps, you can turn a student's disrespect into a memorable lesson. The steps work because they heap the entire burden of responsibility on the student's shoulders, with none of it clinging to you.

He can't blame you or be resentful of you—thus undermining the lesson —because you didn't try to get even. You didn't have to win the battle. You didn't yell, threaten, scold, or lower yourself to the same level of disrespect.

You kept your cool and allowed accountability to work, which is the right thing to do for both you and the student.

26

How to Handle Friendship Drama

φ

FRIENDSHIP DRAMA. The very words can make you shudder. Tears, jealousy, hurt feelings, histrionics, he said/she said . . . although it's the last thing you ever want to deal with, you simply can't ignore it—because it will dominate the lives of whoever is involved to the exclusion of everything else.

It will throw your classroom into upheaval. It will bring your schedule to a halt. It will cause you to waste time pulling students together for powwows, forced apologies, and hash-it-outs. You'll find yourself stuck trying to untangle a laundry list of slights, dirty looks, and misunderstandings, while the business of teaching and learning gets shoved into the background.

But it doesn't have to be this way. What follows are three simple guidelines—or truths about friendships—to help you quickly cut through the muddle and get to the heart of the issue. In doing so, it will bring your students face to face with the consequences of treating friends with anything less than kind respect.

1. You don't have to be friends.

When meeting with students (friends) who aren't getting along, it's important to remind them that as members of your classroom they must treat everyone with respect, best friend and acquaintance alike. It isn't a choice. It's a class rule you will strictly enforce. However, they don't have to be friends. In fact, perhaps they should rethink their friendship. *"If someone isn't nice to you, or is untrustworthy and talking behind your back, then you shouldn't be friends with that person."*

This stops them cold. It is a simple solution they can see right in front of them. But here's the key, where the power lies: Most students don't want to lose friendships, and thus begin to understand that there are consequences for not appreciating them.

2. If you choose to be friends, then be nice.

The next logical extension of guideline number one is that if they want to remain friends, then they have to apologize, forgive each other immediately, and start being nice. *"If you decide to remain friends, then you have to begin this minute being kind to each other."*

It's important that you don't give them another choice in the matter, which is a truism of friendships. They either let bygones be bygones and remain friends, or they don't and go their separate but respectful ways. It's that simple.

3. You can't force someone to be your friend.

If one or more students aren't ready to commit to a renewed friendship, that's okay. You can't force students to be friends, and neither can they force it on each other. True friendship doesn't work that way. *"Although you deserve to be treated with respect, and I want to know if you're not, you can't force anyone to be your friend."*

Here again, what this does is open your students' eyes to the truth that friendships aren't set in stone and should never be taken lightly. They must be nurtured and cherished.

Note: The guidelines are meant to put students on the spot, advance past the hurtful accusations, and get straight to the heart of the matter: Either be nice or dissolve the friendship.

LIFE LESSONS

Our greatest calling as teachers is to impact our students for a lifetime, to be that one teacher they'll always remember—who imparted not just knowledge of reading and writing, but of life lessons they can carry with them into adulthood.

The three guidelines above may seem harsh at first glance, but in practice they are wonderfully compassionate and instructive. They encourage fuller and richer friendships, fewer cliques, and greater sensitivity to how our words and actions affect others. They empower students to seek healthy relationships, and to hold one another accountable for them. They teach the often-overlooked value that simply being nice will fill one's life with true and trusted friends. And they do so in an extremely efficient manner, so you can get back to teaching.

It's important to note that if you teach these guidelines to your entire class, proactively, you'll have few if any friendship problems the rest of the year. No more complaining and arguing. No more tears and dramatics. No more distractions from learning. Just the important, enduring lesson that friendships are special and sacred and are never to be taken for granted.

27

Why Micromanagers Make Bad Teachers

ᗥ

THERE IS A PERVASIVE FEAR in teaching that if you're not on top of your students every moment—coaxing, guiding, advising, directing—you'll lose control of your classroom. If left unchecked, this fear turns otherwise easygoing men and women into micromanagers, hovering over their students like a nervous driver's education instructor.

Skittering like water bugs from one desk to the next, they burst through bubbles of personal space, kneel down hot-breath close, and force their unwanted and unnecessary help upon their students. They comment, advise, opine, and counsel. They warn and praise and interfere. They fret over every this and every that. They recommend and over-assist. They interrupt with yet another itsy-bit of guidance. *"One more thing . . . and one more thing . . . oh, and one more thing . . ."*

No wonder micromanagers feel so stressed, overworked, and exhausted —freefalling into bed at night, backhand across forehead, with a great sigh. *"Ahhhhhhscoobitydoobitydoobitymeemeemeemeemee."*

Yet in spite of all the busyness, the helicoptering, and the hyper-attentiveness, micromanagers struggle mightily with classroom management.

Here's why:

They cause excitability.

Excitability is a major cause of misbehavior, and because it's directly related to how a teacher carries himself (or herself) it's completely avoidable. All the movement and tension and excessive talk micromanagers bring with them to the classroom causes nervous energy that manifests itself in poor listening, poor concentration, and misbehavior.

They show a lack of confidence in their students.

Somewhere deep down, perhaps just beyond conscious awareness, micromanagers don't believe in their students. They don't believe in their students' ability to listen, learn, and follow directions—which is why they give constant input. Sadly, this belief comes across loud and clear to students, who are quick to fulfill their teacher's prophecy.

They suffocate academic and social growth.

No student thrives in a classroom run by a micromanager. The truth is, students need space to learn. They need room to breathe and grow and mature and stand on their own two feet. There are many moments throughout a typical school day when it's best to back off and let students wrestle with their academic work, reflect on their mistakes, and fight their own battles.

They think for their students.

Micromanagers tend to give away answers, solutions, and hints that are far better discovered by their fully capable students—even telling them how to respond in ways that leave nothing to imaginative, creative, or critical thinking. They also frequently paraphrase for students in a manner that suits their own needs and expectations rather than reflecting actual student thought.

They discourage independence.

Micromanagers help students far too much and too often. They're quick to lean down beside individual students to offer endless guidance, interfering with a critical part of the learning process. This causes students to look outside themselves for solutions rather than first attempting to figure them out on their own.

They interrupt learning.

Micromanaging your classroom convinces students that they need more help than they actually do. The fact is, most teachers help too much, talk too much, and are seen too much. After presenting a first-class lesson, and then checking thoroughly for understanding, it's best to fade into the background, allowing your students to think through the challenges you place before them without your added input.

POWERFUL FORCES AT WORK

Knowing when to back off, observe quietly, and let your students work through and apply the tools you've given them to succeed is a little appreciated and often-overlooked aspect of great teaching. It's an art form, to be sure, learned over time by those aware of the powerful forces at work when students are made to realize that, in the end, success and failure resides with them.

Micromanagers steal this wonderful gift from students. By doing too much, by thinking, speaking, and stepping in for their students, they take from them this life-changing realization. They take away the deeply satisfying desire lying—sometimes dormant—within each of us to pull ourselves up by the bootstraps and make something of our often disadvantageous circumstances.

After presenting sharp, clear-cut lessons, the most effective teachers are quick to recede into the background, because they know that when you micromanage students, when you step in, take on, and interfere with what are *their* responsibilities, you rip the heart and soul out of motivation, suppress real, inspired learning, and unleash a torrent of misbehavior.

28

Why Reminders Make Classroom Management More Difficult

ஃ

IF THERE IS ONE classroom management mistake made more often than others, it is the practice of giving reminders *after* misbehavior has already occurred. It's so common, in fact, that it passes the lips of many scores of teachers daily—even hourly—in schools from Fresno to Timbuktu.

"Excuse me . . . excuse me . . . boys and girls? There is no talking when I'm talking."

"Leila, go sit down right now. You know you may not leave your seat whenever you feel like it."

"Anthony and Eric, we don't push in line. You know better than that."

Anytime you spell out for your students what they should or shouldn't be doing—based on behavior standards previously taught—you're giving a reminder. And teachers in the habit of reminding often struggle with classroom management.

Here's why:

It undermines your classroom management plan.

Every time you give a reminder in response to misbehavior, you fail to follow through with your classroom management plan. With no promise of a consequence backing your words, a reminder is nothing more than a suggestion your students can either take or leave—or weigh the merits of based on your mood and the situation.

So naturally when you ask them to line up quietly with their hands at their sides, to them it doesn't really mean you expect them to do it, at least not the first time you ask. If your students know they can count on your repeated reminders before you enforce a consequence, then there is little urgency for them to follow your directions.

It weakens the power of your words.

When your first reaction to misbehavior is to give a reminder, you're communicating to your students that you don't really mean what you say—unless, that is, you raise your voice, lose your cool, or otherwise show your frustration.

There is a direct relationship between the number and frequency of reminders you give and your students' inclination toward listening and doing what you ask.

If you give a lot of reminders, your words won't pack any punch. Your voice will no more cut through the static in their heads than the soft drone of a hummingbird outside your classroom window.

And amidst the resultant daydreaming and boredom is the frequent sting of those who see your weakness as an opportunity to push the limits of your patience.

YOUR WORDS REALIZED

If you just make this one change, if you decide that you're no longer going to give post-misbehavior reminders—and instead follow your classroom management plan as it's written—you will notice dramatic improvement in behavior. Not at first, mind you. Going from multiple reminders to zero will be a shock to the system.

In time, however, the sound of your voice will *matter* to your students. It will have meaning and power and resonance. They'll be tuned in and leaning forward, with a sense of urgency that will allow you to teach with **passion**.

Now when you ask something of your students, you'll see your words materialize in front of you, the dream becoming reality.

29

A Simple Way to Improve Listening

♀

IT'S A COMMON COMPLAINT. You give a direction and nothing happens. Your students just sit there, like they didn't hear a word you said. A few begin moving, perhaps, but slowly, even grudgingly. Others look at each other like, "*Oh, are we supposed to do something?*"

It can feel like you're speaking a different language. And once they do start inching and sighing their way toward doing what you asked, you have to cheer them on like a helicopter parent at a peewee soccer game. You walk or jog alongside, cajoling, gesturing, clapping. You ramp up your energy and enthusiasm. You repeat yourself a half dozen times. *Troy! Troy! Get your head in the game! Troy! Troy! Hey Troy! Troy! Look over here! You can do it! You can do it, superstar! Just run up and kick . . . the . . . ball!*

You get the picture. Do this all day and you'll be ready for a sofa and a cool washcloth over your eyes. Indeed, giving directions to an unresponsive class can make teaching remarkably, exasperatingly stressful. But the solution isn't so difficult. With just a few simple steps you can teach your students to listen and follow your directions the first—and only—time they're given.

Here's how:

Stand in one place.

Find a spot in your room where your students can see you without turning in their seats. Pause there a moment and ask for their attention. You'll not only give your directions from here, but you'll stay in this spot until they're finished following them.

Give your directions once.

After receiving their quiet attention, give the directions you want them to follow *one time,* which is the key to the strategy. Speak in a normal voice, erring on the side of too softly than too loudly.

Let them flounder.

The first time you use this strategy your students may struggle. How much they struggle will be an indicator of how bad things have gotten and how readily they disregard the sound of your voice. Go ahead and let them be confused and unsure of what to do.

Remain motionless.

Resist the urge to jump in and repeat yourself, cajole, or talk them through what you want them to do. Just stand in place and observe. Reveal nothing in terms of what you're doing or why you're doing it.

Let your leaders take over.

Slowly, leaders will emerge to either model for the others what to do or speak up and do the cajoling and repeating for you. This is good. Allow them to take on this responsibility.

Wait.

Don't move or say anything until they're finished following your directions and quiet. Pause for 30 seconds or so to let the lesson sink in.

Give the next direction.

When you're satisfied that all of the science folders are out on their desks, or whatever direction was given, give your next direction. The second time should be noticeably better—faster, sharper, and needing fewer leaders.

Continue giving directions once.

If the second direction went better than the first, then you're on the right track. Go ahead and give another. Eventually, and as long as you're giving directions only one time, you'll be able to increase the complexity.

Make it practice in the beginning.

You may want your first foray into this directions-only-once strategy to be practice. Start slow. Ask your students to do one simple thing, like clear their desks. In time, your students will be able to follow multiple step directions with ease.

If the first time is a disaster . . .

If the first time you try this strategy your students are unable to get it completed (arguing, confusion, disharmony), that's okay. All hope isn't lost. Simply ask for and wait for their attention, then start over from the beginning. They'll get it.

Why It Works

Students become poor listeners when they know they don't *have* to listen. You see, when they know you'll repeat yourself and hold their hand through every direction and every lesson, they have no *reason* to listen.

When they haven't been forced—or even allowed—to think for themselves, when they're unburdened by any responsibility to pay attention, they tune out. They daydream. They let life happen to them. It's human nature.

But when you give directions only one time, and your students know that that's all they're getting, then they learn quite naturally, automatically even, to tune in to the sound of your voice. They learn to listen for what you want.

Each time you use this strategy, which isn't so much a strategy as the way things ought to be, more and more students will come on board. More and more students will become less dependent on you and more dependent on themselves.

Habits will change. Maturity and independence will grow. And listening will become a matter of routine.

30

8 Things Teachers Do to Cause Boredom

♀

WHEN STUDENTS get bored their minds drift, and while some settle on daydreaming, tile-counting, and general inattentiveness, other students are drawn to more . . . ahem . . . destructive pursuits. For where there is boredom, there is misbehavior percolating just under the surface, ready to pounce.

Although there is a lot you can do to counter the onset of boredom, understanding what not to do is the first step to avoiding its negative effects.

What follows is a list of the most common things teachers do to cause boredom. By steering clear of these eight attention killers, your students will spend more time on task and be far better behaved.

1. Sitting too long.

Although it's important to increase your students' stamina for both paying attention during lessons and focusing during independent work, if they're made to sit too long, you're asking for trouble. Good teachers are observant and thus learn to know when to switch gears and get their students up and moving.

2. Talking too much.

Students need room to breathe or they'll form an unspoken mutiny and turn your classroom upside down. Talking too much is especially smothering. It communicates that you don't trust them, teaches them to tune you out, and causes their eyes to glaze over. The more economical and concise you are with your words, the more attentive your students will be.

3. Making the simple, complex.

Many teachers misunderstand the oft-heard mandate for more rigor. They take it to mean that they need to make their instruction more complex, more involved, and more verbose, which is a major reason why students *don't* progress. Our job, if we are to do it well, is to do the opposite. The most effective teachers simplify, break down, and cut away the non-essentials—making content *easier* for students to grasp.

4. Making the interesting, uninteresting.

Most standard grade-level subject matter *is* interesting, but your students don't know that. In fact, many assume, based on their learning experiences in the past, that it's boring. It's your job to show them otherwise. It's your job to give them a reason to care about what you're teaching. So many teachers just talk at their students, forgetting the most critical element: selling it.

5. Talking about behavior instead of doing something about it.

Teachers who struggle with classroom management tend to talk endlessly about behavior. They hold class meetings. They hash things out. They revisit the same tired topics over and over, much to their students' eye-rolling chagrin. Effective classroom management is about action. It's about doing and following through and holding students accountable. It isn't about talking.

6. Directing too much, observing too little.

Most teachers are in constant motion—directing, guiding, handholding, and micromanaging students from one moment to the next. This is not only remarkably inefficient, but it dampens enthusiasm for learning. Instead, rely on sharp, well-taught routines to keep your students awake, alive, and responsible through every transition and repeatable moment of your day, while you observe calmly from a distance.

7. Leading a slow, sloppy, slip-shod pace.

Good teaching strives for a focus and efficiency of time, movement, and energy. The day crackles and glides cleanly from one lesson or activity to the next. As soon as one objective is met, it's on to the next without delay. Moving sharply and purposefully forces students to stay on their toes, their minds engaged. Boredom never enters the picture.

8. Failing to adjust.

Regardless of what you're trying to squeeze in by the end of the day, or how important it seems, the moment you notice heads wilting, you must make an adjustment. It's never worth it to plow through. Sometimes all your students need is a moment to stretch their legs or say hello to a friend. Other times, you'll simply move on to something else.

Learning In The Spotlight

The ability to concentrate over time is a critical and often-overlooked aspect of learning, and so pushing the time-on-task envelop is a good thing.

But there is a fine line, and when students cross that line into boredom, misbehavior is sure to follow. The good news is that by avoiding the common mistakes listed above, you can keep boredom at bay and inspired learning in the spotlight.

31

How to Capture Your Students' Attention

♀

YOUR STUDENTS love video games. They love action movies and bawdy comedies. They love snowball fights, skateboards, birthday parties, and action sports. They love laughter and thrills, challenge and daring-do.

They want to leap off thirty-foot cliffs into murky water below. They want to go on zip-lines, amusement-park rides, and water slides. They want to score the winning goal, hang out with their crazy friends, and eat pizza seven nights a week. They spend their waking moments thinking about, pursuing, or engaging in their desires.

And then they walk into your classroom.

BOREDOM EQUALS MISBEHAVIOR

I know, I know, it's not your job to entertain your students or compete with the excesses of the world. True enough. But if you can't grab their attention and enchant them with your lessons and teaching style, then you're going to lose them to boredom and disinterest.

And as predictable as the rising sun, unengaged students misbehave, break rules, and seek fulfillment in less-than-acceptable ways.

The Classroom Management Secret

Four Desires

The key to capturing your students' attention, and keeping it, is to tap into four desires nearly every student has in abundance.

1. Adventure

Students crave adventure, and if you can give it to them, even in small doses and in vicarious ways, they'll love being in your classroom.

Organize scavenger hunts and walking field trips and outdoor art lessons. Choose read-alouds that transport to other worlds. Act out scenes of scientific discovery. Perform your favorite book passages. Reenact moments in history instead of just reading about them.

Dive headlong into the dramatic stories of adventure behind the yawn-inducing curriculum you've been saddled with. Be wary of the current push in more and more technology, and get your students up and *experiencing* their learning.

2. Humor

Bring regular doses of fun and laughter into your classroom, and your students will follow you to the ends of the earth. Besides storytelling, nothing compares to the rapport-building, behavior-influencing power of humor. Be open to it and you'll find it everywhere you look.

There is no place like a classroom full of kids to find the comically absurd, the notably amusing, and the downright hilarious.

No, you don't have to abandon your rules or waste learning time. The truth is, when your students are happy to be in your class, when they can have a good laugh once in a while, they're less likely to misbehave and more open to learning.

3. Challenge

Among the happiest of people are those whose work challenges them—without it being unreachable, undoable, or discouraging. And this is what you must do with your students. You must continually give them challenges they think they can do, but aren't absolutely sure.

The best way to do this is through provocative questioning: *Who thinks they can teach the class how to perform the experiment? What group wants to try to tackle this problem? Which pair can do this the best, the fastest, or without making a mistake?*

Your job is to know what your students can do so you can ask for a little more, in tempting challenges dangled before them throughout the day.

4. Fascination

This is where your skill as a teacher and showwoman (or showman) comes in. I've found that in every lesson and in every activity there is an opportunity to infuse a dose of fascination and wonderment.

This strategy can be so powerful and can be used in so many different ways, limited only by your imagination. Find the one thing in your lesson that is unique, unusual, magical, shocking, incredible, secretive, special, exclusive, or in some way different and use it to lure your students in.

Now on the surface this one thing might not be very compelling. The trick is to visualize your lesson objectives through the eyes of your students. Find the one thing that stands out and then make it compelling. Make it something your students can't ignore, even if they tried.

Teach To The Heart

If your classroom doesn't include these elements, if you're simply following along with the paint-by-numbers curriculum you've been provided, then classroom management will be a never-ending struggle and academic progress will be teeth-pulling slow.

When you regularly tap into your students' natural desires, however, when you speak and teach directly to their hearts rather than into their ears and over their heads, then their eyes will widen, their backs will straighten in their seats, and they'll be filled with the love of learning.

32

Why a Simple Pause is a Powerful Classroom Management Strategy

⚷

ONE OF THE MOST common errors teachers make when presenting lessons, providing directions, or otherwise addressing students is to string sentences together with very little gap between them. In other words, the teacher will move from one thought, idea, or bit of information to the next without delay, often filling the gaps with *ands*, *ums*, *likes*, and other meaningless words.

It's how most of us speak in our day-to-day life. But the negative effect it can have on students, and on your ability to keep their attention, is substantial.

You see, bridging phrases together without allowing your students time to absorb them makes you uninteresting and difficult to follow. It causes students to turn their attention away from you and toward the daydreams, distractions, and misbehavior opportunities around them.

A simple way to correct this problem, and at the same time become a more effective teacher, is to include frequent, and at times even lengthy, pauses in your speech.

Here's why these little gems of silence are so powerful:

They're predictive.

Anticipating answers and outcomes improves learning, and when you pause, your students will instinctively predict what you're going to say next. You can use this instinct to your advantage by pausing before revealing important ideas, words, theories, or points of emphasis.

They build suspense.

When used strategically, a pause creates suspense and curiosity in the listener, causing them to sit up straighter and lean in closer. It can make the most prosaic information seem interesting and worth listening to—making easier a critical skill many teachers struggle with.

They add depth and drama.

Pausing can be as important as content when presenting lessons. With the right timing and pace—and a bit of attitude—it can infuse your words and the visualizations you create with depth and drama, flair and emotion. It can help bring your curriculum to life, giving it the punch and energy it needs to matter to your students.

They discourage misbehavior.

Speaking without intentional pausing sounds like droning to students, who are quick to lose interest, grow bored, and misbehave. An occasional two or three second pause breaks up the familiar tone of your voice, keeps students on their toes, and helps them stay checked in and on task.

They allow you to adjust.

A pause gives you a moment to quickly assess your students' understanding. It allows you to make eye contact, stay in touch, and make adjustments to your teaching along the way. It trains you to be sensitive to their needs and attuned to their nonverbal reactions to your lessons.

They help your students retain information.

An occasional pause, if for only a second or two, breaks ideas, theories, and directives into chunks, allowing them to sink in before your students are rushed along to the next thing. This improves memory and understanding and gives your students a framework from which to build upon more learning.

IT's THE SIMPLE THINGS

There are no hard and fast rules about when, how often, or how long you should pause. You learn and become better and nimbler at using them through experience. At first, pausing just a couple of seconds may seem like a long time. It may feel strange and uncomfortable, even for your students. But in time, you'll love the impact it has on your teaching.

You'll find yourself speaking with more confidence—using your body and facial expressions more, becoming more dynamic and more willing to take chances with storytelling, playacting, and the like. Your words will have more power. Your lessons will prove more effective. Your students will be more attentive and more interested in you, and less interested in misbehaving.

Like much of classroom management, it is the simple things, when applied consistently, day after day, and perfected over time . . . that add up to great teaching.

33

Why Speaking Softly is an Effective Classroom Management Strategy

⚲

YOU DON'T ALWAYS have to make big, dramatic changes to see classroom management improvement. Sometimes it can be a slight adjustment. A small change in the way you do things, in how you speak, move, or relate to students, can make a big difference.

Your voice is a good example. Most teachers talk too loud. They turn up the volume because they believe that the louder they are the better their students will listen. But it isn't true. Students tune out teachers who bark commands and instructions. To them it sounds like nagging or threatening or that their teacher doesn't think they're bright enough to follow along otherwise. This is one reason why students often grudgingly follow directions, or ignore them altogether.

To encourage good listening, and a *desire* to follow directions, a soft-spoken approach is in order.

Here's why:

Your students will become still.

When you lower your voice, your students will intuitively stop moving so they can hear you. They'll stop fidgeting, tapping, and rustling. They'll stop whispering and twisting in their seats. They'll stop crumbling paper.

They'll stop all the annoying behaviors that frustrate you, interrupt your train of thought, and cause you to repeat yourself.

Your students will lean in and look at you.

It's best to speak just soft enough that the students in the back of the room have to strain ever so slightly to hear you. This way, when you speak, your students will lean in and watch you as you form the words.

Looking at you helps them understand what is being said. It helps them focus on you and your message. When you speak loudly, on the other hand, they're encouraged to look away, move around, and busy themselves with other things.

Your students will want to listen.

When you speak pleasantly and calmly while giving directions, the information goes down a lot smoother. And because it sounds polite, because it sounds like you believe in your students and their ability to listen, you can ask so much more of them.

Like all of us, students appreciate being spoken to with respect. They like being trusted with the information you give them, and not hammered over the head with it. Thus, they'll return the favor by doing what you ask.

Your students will be calmer.

Speaking softly has a calming effect on students. Just by opening your mouth you'll be able to release classroom excitability and nervous tension—which is most often caused by loud, stressed-out, and fast-moving teachers.

A calm, polite voice sends the message that you're in control of the class and that you know exactly what you're doing. This is a comforting, even soothing, notion to students, and it frees them to concentrate on their learning.

Your students will take up your cue.

In many ways a class takes on the personality of their teacher, and if you shout your directions and talk over your students, you'll have a noisy, chaotic classroom.

What you do is more influential than what you say. So when you quiet your voice and speak politely to your students, they'll do the same. They'll use gentler voices and be more respectful when they speak to you, as well as each other.

Tell Them What You Want

Passion and enthusiasm are important to good teaching. So when you're presenting a lesson, motivating your troops, or playing a game with your students, let the moment dictate the volume and intensity of your voice. Cut loose and be the inspirational teacher you were meant to be.

But when you're giving directions, handling behavior issues, and otherwise attending to the day-to-day operations of your class, it's best to dial it down. Stand in one place, look your students in the eye, and speak to them in a soft voice. Tell them exactly what you want.

And they'll give it to you.

34

Why You Should Observe Your Students More and Help Less

♀

MOST TEACHERS don't observe their students enough—because they're too busy meeting with them. They're too busy leaning down to help. They're too busy scurrying from student to student talking them through every this and every that.

They assume that if you don't look like you're working hard, if you're not in some way interacting with students, moving about the room, or reminding your class about *something*, then you must not be very effective. You must not be very good.

But going overboard in helping students doesn't make you a good teacher. In fact, it's a sign of trouble. It's associated with ineffective classroom management, academically immature students, plodding progress, and a chaotic room environment.

Although you may spend some of your time engaged in the activities above, the more you can balance it with quiet, focused observation of your students—while they work independently—the more effective you'll be.

Here's why.

Your students will misbehave less.

Most misbehavior happens when your back is turned, when you're talking, or when you're otherwise busy and distracted with other things. But by observing more, your students will be less inclined to misbehave and more devoted to their responsibilities.

When your central task during independent work time is to observe, rather than moving from one student to the next reteaching what you taught to the entire class minutes earlier, you'll find that few will misbehave so directly and blatantly in front of you.

Your students will become tenaciously independent.

If you're in the habit of helping students immediately following lessons, then you're training them to be dependant on you. You're training them to expect one-on-one reteaching, thus giving them little incentive to pay attention during the initial lesson.

If, on the other hand, you allow your students to noodle the challenges placed before them without your interference, you empower them. You empower them to listen intently, ask smart and relevant questions, and then attack their assigned tasks with confidence.

You'll notice fewer hands in the air, fewer students in real need of assistance, and fewer students falling behind. In other words, by observing more and helping less, your students will become tenaciously independent, even bristling at your suggestions to help.

Your students will accomplish more.

Immediate, focused, and independent practice of *whatever* you teach your students is critical to their success and associated with better learning and faster progress. But you have to get out of their way. You have to step back and allow them to learn.

The results can be remarkable. Their stamina, concentration, and ability to retain information will improve. They'll be able to apply themselves for increasing amounts of time. And you'll find yourself zooming through the curriculum.

You'll know more about your students.

When you make the transition from incessant helping to more observation, you'll find yourself learning and acquiring so much more information about your students.

You'll have an intimate understanding of where they are and where they need to go. Your lessons will become tighter, more efficient, and more finely tailored to their needs. And you'll know precisely how much guided practice to provide before handing over the keys.

What Good Teaching Looks Like

Observation is one of the secrets of good teaching. But it isn't sitting at your desk, idling by, glancing about your room as your students struggle after an uninspired lesson. It's much more than that.

Observation entails an undivided focus on your students—always standing and typically at a distance that allows you to watch your entire class. It also requires you to provide sharp, vibrant lessons, spot-on directions, and prove-it-to-me checking for understanding before releasing them to their work. Otherwise, you won't be free to observe. And your students won't be free of you and the shackles of too much help.

Independent work means not dependent on you. And frequent periods of it—silent, focused, and uninterrupted—isn't too much to ask of any group of students. They really can do it.

An entire class, lost in their work, unaware of the heater clicking on, the scratch and tap of pencils and keyboards, or the brilliant morning sun peeking through the trees outside . . . and you, watching them work, contented but vigilant, knowing that minute by minute and hour by hour they're improving, maturing, and becoming better, more independent students.

It's what good teaching looks like.

35

How to Fuel Your Students' Intrinsic Motivation

♀

MOST STUDENTS are praised too much. They're praised too often, too publicly, and too over-the-top. They're praised for things any reasonable person would conclude are simply not worthy of it. And as the bar of excellence drops lower and lower, it squeezes the work ethic right out of them.

Sure, they smile and blush over their teacher's enthusiastic backslapping. They hold up their pretty certificates for the camera and smooth stickers on the bumper of the family car. But unless the praise was earned, it means nothing. And deep down every student knows it.

Because every time you praise your students for something that didn't involve hard work or a certain mental toughness to accomplish, a sliver of their dignity is taken from them. A soft, sinister voice whispers, *"Pssst! Hey, you in the third row. Yeah, you with the smiley face sticker. You know you didn't really earn it, don't you? Your teacher just gave it to you because average is all you're capable of."*

When teachers refrain from giving praise for doing what is expected, however, and instead keep their eyes pealed for true accomplishment, they add a jolt of fuel to their students' intrinsic motivation. For this kind of praise feeds the churning, unstoppable force that resides in each student, spurring them on to become more than they thought they could. A triumphant voice then shouts from the mountaintops, *"You did it! And you're capable of so much more!"*

What follows are eight ways to give your students intrinsic power through your effective praise.

1. Make it deserved.

Unless the praise you offer is based on achievement, which is defined differently for each student, then it will hold no meaning or have lasting effect. This underscores the importance of knowing your students and their unique abilities, so that when you do see something praiseworthy, you can pounce.

2. Make it subtle.

Small, subtle gestures of praise are among the most effective. Eye contact from across the room, carefully timed, one-word recognition, a single nod of the head—these special moments can send a student's internal motivation into hyper drive.

3. Make it private.

Make your praise a privately shared moment between you and the student. It may seem counterintuitive, but you'll find exclusive praise to have more intrinsic value and greater motivational effect on your students than the over-the-top, public, cheering variety.

4. Make it silent.

You don't always have to make your praise wordless, but doing so can make it especially effective. Quiet applause, fist pumps, winks, knowing smiles, and good old-fashioned handshakes are all wonderful and inherently genuine ways to jump-start your students' intrinsic engines.

5. Make it written.

A stationery note, written in your careful hand, folded over and stuck to the inside of a student's desk is perhaps the most effective form of praise you could offer. If your note is written from the heart, the student will cherish your words—not sharing it with a soul and saving it for years.

6. Make it belated.

Effective praise doesn't have to come immediately following the accomplishment. Sometimes it's best to wait until your praise can be more confidential and unexpected. An out-of-the-blue compliment about which the student didn't even know you noticed can be especially impactful.

7. Make it on potential.

Praise based on untapped ability can provide a much-needed kick in the shorts. When you *know* a student can perform better than he (or she) is showing, give it to him straight. *"As smart as you are, you should be getting A's on your math tests."* Coming from a trusted source like an admired teacher, he'll believe it—and be changed by it.

8. Make it joyous.

Yes, there are times that call for joyous, enthusiastic celebration. But the key here is that it's genuine and that it fits the situation. These spontaneous moments are also best shared with a group of students or, better yet, your entire class.

NOT WITHOUT PRAISE

Just as important as it is to eschew false praise, it's equally important not to let a good work pass without your acknowledgement. Worthy praise is the answer to motivating individual students and getting them to move in the direction you want.

But you can't withhold it. If ever you witness a student stepping beyond what are common expectations and into the realm of true accomplishment, don't let her (or him) hang there on the vine unnoticed, where the fruit of excellence withers and dies. Let her know you noticed. Give her your authentic, intrinsically targeted approval. You'll be amazed at what she's capable of.

More than you ever dreamed.

36

3 Ways You Should Never Praise Students

ၡ

HEARTFELT PRAISE based on true accomplishment is powerful stuff. It feeds your students' internal motivational engines. It spurs them to greater success. It reinforces the slow-to-grow belief that hard work matters, that it really is more than worth the sweat and toil.

Certainly they can see the proof of its fruits without your acknowledgement—sharper skills, higher competence, deeper confidence. But shining a light on their accomplishments can heighten the experience, making it lasting and more impressionable.

Good teaching requires that you keep an eye out for excellence, effort, or achievement beyond what is commonly expected. It calls for you to praise artfully, choosing the right tone, timing, and mode to match the student and the situation. Although a thoughtful, subtle response is often best, there are times when a spontaneous reaction is just right—one bursting with joyous pride in your students and their successes.

Too many teachers, though, praise not out of genuineness, not out of a pure motive to highlight hard-earned achievement or excellence, but out of their own desires. What follows are three ways you should never praise students, for not only are they ineffective beyond several minutes, but they're more about the teacher and his or her wants and needs than they are about the student.

1. For personal gain.

In this scenario, the teacher praises an individual student for the sole purpose of placating or subduing his or her behavior. It's done proactively and dishonestly. You see this over and over again, often all day long, with difficult students.

"Great job so far today, Anthony. Keep it up, partner!"

The student is praised not in response to any valid improvement, success, or accomplishment, but rather in an effort to mollify, satisfy, appease, and otherwise keep in check for as long as possible. In other words, the purpose of the praise is to benefit the teacher.

2. In order to manipulate.

This form of praise is used to manipulate an entire group of students into compliant behavior. The way it works is that the teacher will choose one student to praise for *expected* behavior with the hope that it will cause others to do the same.

"Wow, I sure like how David is sitting. Way to go!"

Often called "caught being good," this too is disingenuous. The teacher isn't *really* impressed with David. After all, sitting appropriately is an expectation and not in any way an accomplishment. The teacher is using David as a pawn to get what he or she wants.

Note: An honest way to influence other students would be to simply thank David for sitting appropriately.

3. **Out of obligation**.

Most teachers have been told time and again that they can't praise students too much or too enthusiastically. So they let 'em have it every chance they get. Upon seeing behavior that *isn't* poor, they pounce.

"Good job, Karla! You found a library book just like I showed you!"

They keep at it because they think that that's what good teachers do. And along the while, true and beautiful accomplishment passes beneath their noses either unnoticed or praised with the same insincerity one receives after finding a library book.

WORTHY PRAISE ONLY

All three examples above are forms of false praise. That is, they're ways of praising students based on something other than true accomplishment. The problem with false praise is that it lowers the standard of what is good. It communicates unmistakably that fulfilling the barest minimum is not only good enough, but somehow special.

It places what is good and lovely and exceptional on the same local theatre marquee of what is commonly expected—instead of where it belongs: in lights on Broadway. A deeply moving poem, then, chiseled and shaped through hours of dedicated work, gets the same reaction from the teacher as does sitting up straight in one's chair.

For praise to mean something, for it to help *change* behavior, inspire excellence, and fuel a dream of becoming the next E.E. Cummings or Emily Dickinson, it must be worthy. It must be genuine and real and come from the stirrings in your heart. It must be a moment in time, a shared recognition, a soulful celebration of a step beyond where your students have ever been before.

Note: True accomplishment varies from student to student and can only be discerned through the keen eyes of an observant teacher.

37

Why You Should Never, Ever Be Friends With Students

⚿

ONE OF THE KEYS to effective classroom management is to build relationships with students. Making personal connections—through humor, kindness, likability, and more—is a powerful way to influence behavior. It can also be astonishingly rewarding. The give-and-take with students, the trusting rapport, the shared affection—these are the things that make teaching more than just a job.

But there is a danger in building relationships with students. There is a line that can never be crossed. If you try to connect with students on their level, in a peer-to-peer-like friendship, then your efforts to influence their behavior will backfire.

Here's why:

They won't respect you.

Your students need someone to look up to, not a buddy to hang out with. You're not a peer and therefore should never behave like one. When you use slang or try to be hip or become overly familiar, they'll lose respect for you. Your influence comes from your position as their teacher, not their friend.

They'll stop listening to you.

Becoming too informal or casual in your interactions with students will weaken the power of your words. The urgency for your students to listen and learn will wane as the year rolls on and more of them begin wearing a too-cool-for-school attitude.

They'll challenge you.

As soon as your students get a whiff of your "cool teacher" vibe, they'll start challenging and testing you. And you'll likely find yourself in a showdown with a few or more students bent on wresting control of the classroom from you.

Rules will no longer apply.

Your students will react to your buddy-buddy management style by routinely and nonchalantly breaking your rules. They'll stand and approach you in the middle of a lesson. They'll stop raising their hand. They'll assume, since you are friends, that the rules don't really apply to them.

Consequences are taken personally.

Your students will start reacting to being placed in time-out by blaming you. They'll become hurt and angry with you for merely doing what you said you would. Some may even pout, have a mini temper tantrum, or refuse to talk to you.

Accountability no longer works.

Accountability only works when students acknowledge internally that they indeed made a mistake. So if when sitting in time-out they're mad at you because they feel you betrayed them by putting them there, then there is no accountability and no motivation to improve their behavior.

You become lax with your classroom management plan.

Because your students tend to act dramatically when given a consequence, you will naturally begin to shy away from following your classroom management plan. You'll tiptoe around them. So instead of *you* having leverage to influence their behavior, they'll now have leverage with you.

TIPS FOR BUILDING INFLUENCE

Building influential relationships with students without confusing them about who you are and what your role is isn't difficult. Follow the tips below, and you'll be the teacher they need instead of the friend who disappoints them.

- Be a teacher, mentor, and role model, but never a friend.
- Maintain a polite but warm level of professional distance.
- Engage in the same friendly banter with all students.
- Don't use slang or terms popular with them.
- Model politeness and expect it in return.
- Decline any and all offers to be Facebook friends.
- Follow your classroom management plan as it's written, the same for every student in your class.
- Focus on creating a classroom your students love coming to every day.

Influence that is powerful enough to get your students to *want* to behave and *want* to learn is not born of peer-like friendship, casualness, or laid-back coolness. It is born of likability and respect.

If your students like you because you're friendly and good-humored, and they respect you because you always do what you say you're going to do, then your influence will grow naturally.

38

How to Make Your Classroom a Safe Haven for Your Students

⚷

WE KNOW about the public cases, those gossiped about so offhandedly —the homeless student, the one whose mother is in jail, the two with drug dealing fathers no longer around.

But what of the others? What of the secrets hidden and locked away, keys all but resting on an ocean floor? What about the shy boy seated near the front who won't look you in the eye? He appears well taken care of— clean clothes, hair moussed, new sneakers. But what you don't see is waiting for him at home. What you don't see are the drunken rants, the assaults on his self-worth, and the emotional pain he carries with him like a war wound.

The truth is, despite our vigilance, we don't know what happens when our students leave our classroom. We don't know of the hurt, the fear, and the sadness some wear slung over their shoulders like a heavy backpack.

They put on a good face, these heroic students, and bury their secrets well. And although we can't always know the challenges they face, we can make sure our classroom is a welcome shelter from the storm. We can make sure our classroom is a place where our students can exhale and know they're loved, wholly protected, and free to learn and enjoy school without looking over their shoulder.

Here's how:

Rely on schedules, routines, and procedures.

Knowing what is expected of them during every moment of the school day is a great comfort to students. It allows them to let down their guard and get lost in the steady pace and flow of a well-run classroom. As much as possible, follow the same daily schedule and rely on well-taught routines and procedures.

Maintain a clean, organized classroom.

An attractive room environment speaks volumes to your students about how you value respect, work habits, and expected behavior. When they enter your classroom they should feel as if they're walking into a world that makes sense, in stark contrast to the choppy, churning waters many navigate during their daily lives.

Be the same teacher yesterday, today, and tomorrow.

Inconsistency in word, behavior, or action is confusing to students and will deeply affect their trust in you. It causes resentment, low motivation, and misbehavior. It also brings tension and unhappiness to your classroom and sends the message that you're yet another adult that can't be counted on.

Be kind.

It's so simple but means so much. Treat every student with kindness, patience, and gentleness, regardless of how difficult at times that can be. Doing this one thing will send your likability through the roof and allow you to build easy rapport with your students.

Protect your students from misbehavior.

This is key to creating a classroom your students look forward to coming to every day. They must feel safe and comfortable working with and sitting next to any and all of their classmates. Every day they come to school they should feel confident in knowing that they'll be able to enjoy their day without being interrupted, bothered, or bullied.

Don't take misbehavior personally.

Teachers who yell, threaten, use sarcasm, or otherwise take misbehavior personally are disliked and distrusted intensely—though often privately—by students. They're also *least* likely to follow a classroom management plan, which would allow them to demand the highest standards of behavior without causing friction with students.

Maintain a peaceful learning environment.

Few students do well in a tension-filled classroom, but those with difficult lives outside of school have a particularly rough time—often shutting down, staring off into space, or engaging in serious misbehavior. A classroom is only as peaceful as the teacher in charge. You set the tone with your calm presence, even reactions, and pleasant attitude.

A SAFE HAVEN

The world is becoming more seductive and more dangerous to our students than ever before, all but dragging them away from the academic skills, moral character, and standards of behavior they need to lead meaningful, successful lives. But we can fight back.

We *can* compete with the excesses of the world. We *can* help our students overcome their sometimes awful, painful home lives.

When you make exceptional classroom management your top priority, you're not only able to create the classroom *you* really want, but you're able to create one that's best for your students.

You're able to create a classroom they love being part of and look forward coming to every day, a classroom where they can build genuine friendships, grow responsible and independent, and accelerate academically. You're able to create a classroom free of worry, fear, and negative stress.

You're able to create a safe haven for your students.

39

What to Do When You Realize You've Lost Control of Your Class

ዋ

MAYBE IT'S THE MOMENT you find yourself talking over your students, raising your voice just to be heard above the din. Maybe it's while in the midst of another lesson spiraling into disorder. Maybe it's the flash of recognition upon locking eyes with a favorite student—a sadness behind the soft smile, a weariness from the interruptions and wasted time.

At some point you have to face reality. You have to shake yourself to your senses and realize that no, you don't just have a tough class. It's not because you work in a certain neighborhood. It's not the parents, society, video games, or lack of administrative support. No, the problem is that you've lost control of your class.

But once you come to grips with this realization, once you decide you no longer want to teach in a stressful, chaotic environment, you can start doing something about it.

The plain truth is, you can gain control of your classroom anytime you want to. In fact, with the following strategy you can walk into *any* classroom and have the students calm and following your directions within 30 minutes.

Here's how:

The Classroom Management Secret

Step 1: Take a stand.

The first step is to get your students seated and quiet, but because you've probably lost respect right along with your control, this in itself may be no easy task. Just asking them is unlikely to result in anything but casual compliance.

So what do you do? You do what you have to do. This may entail calmly repeating *"Please return to your seats"* over and over again. It may require you to walk around the room asking and shooing individual students to their desks. It may take five minutes of pleading. Whatever the case, while you're doing this humiliating work, resolve to never put yourself in this position again. Resolve to never again let your class slide to such a degree that you all but have to beg them to do what you ask.

Once you have your students seated, have them clear their desks so there are no distractions, and then simply ask them to be quiet. Tell them you want no talking. Pause for 30-seconds or so and then ask again. Continue in this manner until they are indeed quiet.

Now just wait. Don't move around the room or busy yourself with other work. Your students, their education, and gaining control of your class are your only priorities. How long you'll need to wait depends on how out of control your class has become. But because your students aren't getting much out of your teaching the way things are, you need to be willing to wait as long as it takes.

If you follow the advice above, and you're careful not to show outward frustration, it typically doesn't take long. Once your students are quiet, I recommend waiting in silence another five minutes after the last voice is heard.

You want to send the message that business is no longer usual. You're taking a stand—finally—for them, for you, for everyone who ever told you that you can't manage students in this school or in that neighborhood or without yelling, berating, and being someone you loathe to be.

It's important to point out that you too should remain silent during this time. You shouldn't explain yourself or why they're having to sit and wait. Letting them figure it out on their own is one reason why the strategy works.

Step 2: Do one thing well.

During this second and final step you're going to lay the foundation for how you want your students to behave from this point on.

The best place to start is with a common routine. For most classrooms, lining up to leave the room is the perfect routine because it happens every day and there are multiple opportunities for misbehavior. It's also a routine that transfers to other routines, procedures, tasks, and activities. In other words, if they can line up well, they can do just about anything else well too.

Again, without explaining yourself, and with as few words as possible, model for your students how you want them to line up. Just jump right in: *"When I say 'go' you're going to line up at the door. Here is how you're going to do it."*

Be sure and model in a way that makes you ideally happy. In other words, if you could wave a magic wand and have your students line up in any way you want, what would it look like? Calm? Quiet? Polite? Arms at their sides, facing forward, with a foot of space between? Aim for the stars, because the truth is you really can have it any way you want.

After asking if there is anyone who *doesn't* know what to do, give them a chance to practice. Chances are they'll line up better this first time than they ever have before. Regardless, if it isn't perfect—and you'll do well to find something amiss—send them back to their seats to try again.

Remember, you're sending a message. It's an intervention of sorts. You're turning your classroom upside down, shaking it, and beginning anew. You're restoring order to a place fallen into chaos and disrespect. If it takes 20 minutes of practice to perfect lining up, then so be it.

SHOW ME

You now have a single block upon which you can start building something special. And building upon that one success, you can build another, and another. A classroom of learning and kindness and respect is built one routine, one lesson, and one moment at a time. One after another.

The next time you get the slightest suspicion that the train is running loose upon the rails, ease down steady and fast on the brakes. Bring every moving piece of your classroom, even the clock on the wall, to a standstill.

Send your students back to their desks. Wait until you have their attention and respect.

And then make them prove themselves once again.

40

How to Press the Restart Button on Classroom Management

♀

ONE OF THE HAPPY TRUTHS about classroom management is that you can always press the restart button. You can always call a do-over. Any time you like.

So as soon as you notice your students becoming less motivated and more prone to misbehavior, that's exactly what you should do. Crumble up and start over. Don't wait until your students are climbing the walls and you're sobbing during your lunch break. Do it now.

Every day your wet finger should be in the air, testing the behavioral winds of your classroom. If you don't like the direction they're blowing, it's time to shake things up and start over from scratch.

Here's how:

Begin first thing in the morning.

It's best to start over in the morning, as soon as your students arrive to school. In the meantime, if you're trying to get through a rough afternoon, slow everything down. Take your time, talk less, and wait until your students are quiet and looking at you before moving on to the next thing.

Rearrange seating.

Before your students arrive in the morning, change the seating arrangement, as well as where students sit in relation to one another. A new place to sit signals to students that change is in the air. The old way of doing things isn't in play any longer.

Clean up the clutter.

Physical environment has a noticeable effect on behavior. A tidy, clean look, with lots of pride and open space, sparks an immediate understanding in students—without you saying a word—that excellence is expected. Clutter, on the other hand, whispers to all who enter your classroom, *"Mediocre will do."*

Block out one hour (or more).

Most teachers are in a hurry to plow through the curriculum, giving less attention to the one thing that makes the greatest difference in the classroom: classroom management. Clear your schedule for first thing in the morning. Give yourself at least one hour to work your classroom back into shape.

Model procedures first.

Your students need to know exactly what to do and how to do it well during every minute of the school day. When they don't, bad things happen. Routines and procedures are critical to your success—and sanity. They should be reviewed, modeled, and practiced during the first half of your one-hour block.

Practice walking in line.

Although all procedures are important, walking in line is at the top of the list. Nothing focuses students faster or more effectively than practicing a smooth, brisk, arrow-straight line. It gets them doing things the right way, which will then transfer to everything they do.

Reintroduce your classroom management plan.

After practicing procedures, your students will be calmer, more attentive, and more receptive to your instruction. Now is the time to reintroduce your classroom management plan. Model each rule and consequence like it's the first day of school.

Recommit yourself.

If your students have become careless with their behavior, then you've become careless with classroom management. It's as simple as that. So own up to it. Tell your students that you've done a poor job of holding them accountable and therefore haven't fulfilled your most important job: to protect their right to learn without interference. Then give your word that it won't happen again.

PEDAL TO THE METAL

Whenever you feel like you're losing control of your classroom, it's because of something you're doing—or not doing. It's not about your students. It never has been and it never will be. It's about you.

Effective classroom management is a daily, hourly, commitment. As soon as you let up and relax your standards, you're going to pay for it—with interest.

The solution is to keep your foot on the gas, propelling your students toward your ever-rising bar of excellence. Do this, and you'll never have to start over.

41

How to Improve Classroom Management by Doing Less

ǂ

IT'S NATURAL for teachers struggling with classroom management to try to do more. They talk more, move around the room more, and meet with students more. They race through lessons hoping to finish before losing students to the hum and distraction of a rowdy class. They create another chart, try out another incentive, and have another go at behavior contracts.

Before long, they become so accustomed to the frenetic pace that it becomes normal, the cost of being a teacher. But what else is there to do but something more?

DOING LESS EQUALS MORE CONTROL

Take a deep breath . . . if you slow down, move less, talk less, and at times do absolutely nothing, you will gain more control—and classroom management won't be such a challenge.

Here's how to do less:

Slow down.

It's always smart to take your time. If you rush or get ahead of your students, you'll lose them—and control of your class. By slowing down, you'll cover more material, bring peace to your classroom, and have better behaved students.

Move less.

You've probably been told that teachers should move around the room a lot and avoid staying in one place. But this is poor advice. Your students need to focus on you and your instruction and nothing else. This is best accomplished by staying in one place. There should be no misunderstanding about where their eyes, ears, and thinking ought to be.

Talk less.

Most teachers talk too much. The reality is, the more you talk, the less your students will tune in and the more likely they are to misbehave. If you want your words to have meaning and impact, be brief, get to the point, and move on. Save your voice for inspired lessons, readings, stories, and activities.

Pause often.

Whenever you speak to your class, pause often. Allow a beat or two of silence between sentences. This helps students focus on your message, allows them to process what you've told them, and gives you a chance to see how well they're following along.

Do nothing.

If your students aren't giving you what you want, stop whatever you're doing, stand in the most prominent place in your classroom, and do nothing. When your students are silent and looking at you, wait some more.

Gather your thoughts. When you're ready, tell them again precisely what you expect and then have them do it again.

Lower your voice.

When you raise your voice, you train your students to listen to you only when you get loud and to tune you out the other times. It says, "Okay, I'm yelling because I really mean it this time!" If you want your students to listen, speak softly. They should have to lean forward ever so slightly in order to hear you.

Trust your classroom management plan.

You created a classroom management plan for a reason. So use it. Let it do the heavy lifting. Pull yourself away from the drama and frustration of trying to plead, persuade, intimidate, and bribe your students into behaving. These methods, all examples of trying to do more, don't work.

A New You

Decide today that you're going to start doing things differently. Gone are the days of trying to do more, of chasing trends, of being stressed and in a hurry, of hoping your students will behave. Instead, decide that you're going to do what really works.

Students respond predictably to certain teacher behaviors. You can't just wing it. You can't just do what comes naturally or what feels right. More than any other area of teaching, effective classroom management requires you to work smarter, not harder.

This is a perfect example. Rather than doing more and having little to show for it, do less and become more effective.

42

6 Personality Traits That Make Classroom Management More Difficult

ę

IF YOU'RE STRUGGLING with classroom management and wondering why, one of the first areas to examine is the personality you bring with you to the classroom. Many teachers become different people the minute their students walk through the door.

Sometimes this is a good thing—if being around students makes you brighten like a Broadway singer or become as preternaturally calm as a mountain lake.

But for the vast number of teachers, the presence of a large and active group of students can, at least to some degree, bring about personality traits that are detrimental to classroom management success.

The good news is that with a simple two-minute routine you can condition yourself to eliminate those traits that work against you, and replace them with those that work in your favor.

The following six teacher personality traits make classroom management more difficult. You'll do well to leave them outside your classroom door.

The Classroom Management Secret

1. Impatience

Impatient teachers talk fast, move fast, and tend to either look the other way in the face of misbehavior or react emotionally to it. They rush through lessons, gloss over instructions, and out of necessity have lower expectations for students. This produces a restless, excitable classroom that is primed to cause trouble.

2. Quick To Anger

A single flash of anger can undo weeks of rapport building with your students. When you yell, scold, use sarcasm, or otherwise lose your cool, you distance yourself from your students and undermine their trust and respect of you. You become less approachable, less likable, and less influential—all critical keys to creating a well-behaved classroom.

3. Pessimism

Teachers who are pessimistic in nature are unable to create the well-behaved classroom they desire. Negative thoughts, feelings, and attitudes about students—particularly difficult students—are impossible to hide. They reveal themselves through your words, body language, and tone of voice and make building relationships an awkward struggle.

4. Irritability

Irritability (grouchiness, moodiness) communicates to students that they can't trust you or depend on you. It creates resentment, confusion, and instability. It also causes you to be inconsistent, both with your classroom management plan and in your interactions with students, leading to more frequent and more severe misbehavior.

5. Overly Sensitive

Teachers with thin skin inevitably, and often subconsciously, seek revenge against their students. They can't help themselves. Out of their resentment and spite they make the kind of classroom management mistakes like yelling, scolding, and holding grudges that result in a downward spiraling of student behavior.

6. Easily Frustrated

Frequent sighs, rolling eyes, red-faced lectures—outward signs of frustration can cause enveloping, knife-cutting tension in your classroom. When you allow students to get under your skin, it not only makes your classroom unnerving and unpleasant, but it causes students to challenge your authority and test you whenever they get the chance.

A SIMPLE TWO-MINUTE ROUTINE

The way you present yourself to your students has a monumental effect on classroom management—more so than most teachers realize. If you're at all susceptible to one or more of the personality traits above, then you'll be a more effective teacher if you get a handle on them.

The simplest way is to spend a couple of minutes before your students arrive each day with your eyes closed, visualizing your best self calmly and confidently managing your classroom. Picture yourself responding to misbehavior with poise. Watch as you joyfully present your lessons to a responsive class. See yourself building rapport, loving your job, and following your classroom management plan to the letter.

When you choose to see only the best in yourself and in your students, when you lock the image of your perfect teaching experience in your head and refuse to let it go . . . then that's exactly what you'll get.

43

Why You Should Never, Ever Yell at Students

ę

IN THIS DAY AND AGE it's critical that you become an expert in classroom management—because if you don't, dealing with an unruly class can be maddening. It's easy to lose your cool. It's easy to become the kind of teacher you never wanted to become.

And when you do, when you yell, scold, and wag your finger, you're often rewarded with immediate improvement. A thorough dressing-down can stop misbehavior in its tracks. But the price is exorbitantly high. Yelling is a costly mistake.

Here's why:

Improvement is temporary.

Yelling only works in the moment. Like a playground bully, it's used to intimidate students into compliance. The only reason why it works is because the teacher has an unfair size and/or authority advantage.

It doesn't change behavior.

Behavior only changes when students *want* to behave better, which is the result of unwavering accountability combined with a teacher they like and trust. In the end, yelling causes more misbehavior, not less.

It weakens your influence.

Yelling will cause students to dislike you, distrust you, and desire to disrupt your class. Let's face it, even one revengeful student can make your life miserable. You need your students on your side.

It replaces real accountability.

Teachers who yell tend to do so instead of following their classroom management plan. Students learn quickly that if they can endure their teacher's outburst, they can be on their way without being held accountable.

It sabotages real accountability.

Teachers who lecture, yell, or scold while escorting students to time-out, drive a wedge through the teacher/student relationship, causing anger and resentment. So instead of sitting in time-out and reflecting on their mistakes, your students will be seething at you.

It causes students to tune you out.

When you yell, you train your students to listen to you only when you raise your voice. In other words, they learn that unless you're shouting, you must not really mean it. Before you know it, you'll be giving directions like a carnival sideshow barker.

It's stressful.

Yelling is a sure sign that you let misbehavior get under your skin. It's an expression of frustration, of taking behavior personally, and of trying to get even with students. It's also terribly stressful. It's bad for your health. And it makes teaching a cheerless slog.

It's difficult to defend.

Yelling at students is near the top of the list of parent complaints. And it's difficult to defend. "I'm sorry, I just lost my cool" is about the best you can do. The fact is, no misbehavior, and no level of disrespect, warrants yelling at students.

It's graceless.

Have you ever seen yourself on video losing your cool? Probably not, but one thing is for sure: it ain't pretty. You might as well grab a megaphone and shout, "Hey everybody—students, fellow teachers, administration—I don't have control of my class!"

It provides a poor model.

Students are more influenced by what you do than by what you say. When you yell, react emotionally to misbehavior, or otherwise lose your composure, you provide a poor model for your students for how to behave when things don't go their way.

INSTEAD OF YELLING...

No matter how frustrated you may get with your students, yelling should never be an option. Although it often works in the moment, the cost is much too high. So instead of being *that* teacher, the one with the reputation for yelling and for "being mean," why not be the one that every student wants as their teacher? Why not be the one students respect, admire, and enjoy learning from?

To start, create a classroom management plan that is fair to all students and stick with it. Then put the easy-to-use strategies you learn in this book into action and create a learning experience both you and your students love coming to every day.

44

How to Repair a Broken Relationship With Your Students

⚷

SO YOU LOST your cool. You raised your voice. You put your students in their place. You stomped around in a huff and behaved in a manner you're not proud of. You said things you wish you could take back.

And now as the school day draws to a close, guilt gnaws at your conscience. You smile sweetly and bid your students goodbye as they file out of the room. But it's clear something in them has changed, like an innocence lost or a disappointment found. They leave without looking back.

You close the door and lock it. You find your way to your desk and slump into your chair. You cradle your head in your hands. *What have I done? Did I just ruin everything?*

Breaking your students' trust and damaging the rapport you've worked so hard to establish may indeed feel like the end of the world. But students are remarkably forgiving. And with the right approach, you can always draw them back into your circle of influence.

Here's how:

Wait until tomorrow.

It's best to wait until the next morning before addressing the incident that precipitated your outburst. Give yourself and your students a fresh start, a chance to view each other through the lens of a brand new day.

Admit your mistake.

As soon as your students are settled, tackle the situation head-on. Say simply, "Yesterday I was unhappy with the way you behaved during math, and I handled it poorly. I lost my cool and I'm sorry."

Note: Apologizing is as much for you as for them. It also provides a model for your students and is the quickest way to right the ship.

Let it sink in.

After your brief but direct apology, give your students a moment to let it sink in. A pause will also keep you from going on and on and diluting the impact of your words. The idea is to make amends quickly, impressionably, and without fuss.

Don't let them off the hook.

Now is your opportunity to do what you should have done instead of losing your cool. Hold your students accountable for the previous days' behavior by having them redo whatever it is that caused your, ahem, moment of weakness.

Avoid fun and games.

Resist the urge to try to win them back with a fun afternoon, a silly game, or an easing of your behavior standards. These methods are manipulative. They hold no meaning for students and will cheapen your relationship with them.

Take it slow.

Trust is built over time with your consistent behavior. It's an hour-by-hour, day-by-day sameness that restores rapport and influence. Be pleasant, don't try too hard, and respond to every act of misbehavior with calm accountability. You'll win them back before you know it.

Learn from it.

We all make mistakes. It's what you do with them that matters and makes the difference in the teacher you become. Resolve to use yours as an opportunity to learn and to get better and to leapfrog into greater understanding.

KEEPING COOL

One of the keys to keeping your cool is to never let behavior reach the point where it gets under your skin. If *ever* you see something you don't like, either stop your class in their tracks, show them what you expect, and then make them do it again or, in the case of individual students, simply follow your classroom management plan.

Far too many teachers accept a little pushing here, a little side-talking there, allowing their students to only sort-of follow their classroom rules and directives.

Sure, they'll remind and warn and complain until their throat hurts, but they never actually do anything about it. They just endure it, which over time is bound to get the best of them, bound to cause them to do or say something they'll regret. Maybe even every day.

Setting the bar where you *really* want it, though, and then holding students accountable for reaching it, not only keeps you cool and happy under the collar, but it allows you to maintain the kind of influential relationships with your students that are critical to your—and their—success.

45

5 Ways to Be a Calmer, More Effective Teacher

ᑯ

YOUR TEMPERAMENT has a strong impact on student behavior. If you have a tendency to become tense, stressed, or uptight around your students, then they're far more likely to misbehave—because a tightly wound teacher translates to a tension-filled classroom, the kind of tension visitors can feel tingling in their sensory receptors the moment they enter your classroom.

And make no mistake, tension is bad for classroom management, causing students to become excitable, unfocused, and primed to cause trouble. The good news is that it isn't difficult to change. It isn't difficult to approach each new day of teaching with a calm, unruffled sense of purpose —dissipating tension like a lifting fog reveals a sunny day.

Here's how:

Decide.

Maintaining a calm attitude throughout your teaching day is a choice you make *before* your students arrive. So every day, sometime prior to the morning bell, give yourself a moment of peace to sit quietly at your desk. Take a few deep breaths and relax into your chair.

Now decide that no matter what happens that day, no matter how crazy or how alarming, **you will not** lose your composure. And guess what? You won't. This technique, employed by scores of professional athletes needing to perform at their best, seems almost too easy. But it's remarkably, inexplicably, effective.

Slow down.

By slowing your movements to an easier-going, more graceful pace, your mind will slow down as well—becoming less distracted, more observant, and better able to respond to your students.

You don't have to move like a Tai Chi master or in any way dampen your enthusiasm. It's more of a reminder not to get caught up frenetically shuffling papers, pacing a groove in the floor, or racing mindlessly from one task to another, as so many teachers are wont to do.

Speak calmly.

When giving directions, providing information, and responding to your students, it pays to speak calmly. It soothes nervous energy, helps students focus on you and your message, and gives them confidence that what you say is important and worth listening to.

During lessons, however, all bets are off. You might find yourself whispering with wide-eyed fascination one moment and giving an oration like James Earl Jones the next. Calmness on inside doesn't mean passionless or moribund on the outside.

Breathe.

It's remarkable what a few long, slow breaths can do. Almost immediately, blood pressure drops, your expression softens, and tension drains from your body. By taking a couple of deep breaths every hour, you'll exhale the tension and excitability right out of your classroom.

Oxygen provides vital energy and brainpower. And when you become aware of your breathing, you'll not only calm your own nerves, sharpen your mental acuity, and brighten your state of mind, but you'll become a calming and centering influence on your students.

Prepare.

You may have heard it said that it's physically impossible to be nervous if your body remains relaxed. This may be true, but it's far easier said than done. Relax the mind, however, and the body is sure to follow.

A simple, real-world way to do this is to be mentally prepared. Take several extra minutes to review your lesson plans. Visualize how the day will proceed. See yourself responding to your students with poise, dignity, and calm assuredness.

Calming Waters

Excitability in students is a major source of misbehavior, and in nearly every circumstance, teachers are to blame. Perpetually busy, racing thoughts, under the gun, unsure, unprepared, stressed-out. These common teacher behaviors create tension in the classroom and push students' buttons like almost nothing else.

It makes them feel like they're forever clicking to the top of a roller coaster, anticipating a drop that never comes. They can't sit still. They can't pay attention. And all they want to do is squirm, chat, play, and roughhouse

—anything but listen to you.

But you have the power to fix it. You have the power to calm the stirred waters of your classroom. It takes nothing more than a new way of thinking, a simple turn of the wheel, a change of direction.

And it's smooth sailing ahead.

46

The Ideal Attitude for Exceptional Classroom Management

§

ONE OF THE MOST common email questions I get is, "What about students from disadvantaged backgrounds?" The question never ceases to knock me back on my heels because, truth be told, every strategy on the Smart Classroom Management website and in this book has been developed in classrooms with students living in the most challenging circumstances. Disadvantaged, crime-ridden, poverty-stricken, you name it.

The fact is, it doesn't matter where you teach or who shows up on your roster, the well-behaved classroom you long for is within your grasp. But there is an obstacle blocking the path of so many teachers in their quest for their dream class: a negative attitude.

For if you don't believe it's possible to transform your class, if your default setting is to point the finger at outside circumstances, if you're in the habit of bemoaning the make up of your classroom or the neighborhood you teach in, then it will never happen for you. A defeatist point of view will undermine everything you do, sealing your fate to a career of frustration, disappointment, and dissatisfaction.

What follows are seven principles that form the ideal attitude for exceptional classroom management. Adopt them for yourself, and in the words of Thoreau, you'll "meet with a success unexpected in common hours."

You have to believe it.

In order to create the class you really want, you have to believe deep down that you can—not merely as a possibility, but as a foregone conclusion that you will. Decide right now to seize hold of that image you have of your perfect teaching experience. Keep the image locked clear and vivid in your mind, believing in it and not letting it go until it materializes in front of you.

You have to believe in them.

So many teachers are defeated before ever getting started because they look at their students and think, *there is no way this group can ever be the class I really want.* But as soon as you make that false determination for yourself and your students, all hope is lost. Instead, choose to see only the best in your students. Think only in possibilities. Focus only on what you hope them to be—and then make it happen.

You have to stop making excuses.

It's easy to view the challenging and sometimes appalling home lives of students as an excuse for poor behavior. It's easy to blame parents, the neighborhood, and even the school itself for the chaos of your classroom. They are among the many ready-made scapegoats you can drag out whenever you need them. But the truth is, offering excuses, even in the privacy of your own mind, is akin to giving up on your students—as well as on yourself.

You have to take responsibility.

Regardless of how difficult it may seem, you must take responsibility for both the successes and failures in your classroom. Whether you are or aren't directly responsible for this incident or that disruption is irrelevant. Take ownership anyway. By taking responsibility for everything within the four walls of your classroom, you instantly become a better, more effective teacher.

You have to commit to doing what is right.

You won't always feel like enforcing consequences, being a stickler for polite behavior, or ensuring routines are done properly. There will be moments when you'll have an overwhelming desire to let things go. But you must make the hard decisions, even when it's the last thing you want to do, even when it seems no harm will come by looking the other way, even when it is the last minute of the last day of school.

You have to ignore the squawking birds.

There is no shortage of teachers willing to line up to tell you why you can't create the class you really want. Commiserating over the perceived hopelessness of the job is a favorite feel-better pastime in teacher lounges and lunchrooms the world over. If you're willing to listen, you'll get 101 reasons why you can't do this or that with *those* students. But none of it is true. True for them perhaps, but not for all, and certainly not for you.

You have to become a student of classroom management.

All students behave predictably to certain teacher behaviors and classroom management principles. Stick to what works, and you will succeed. But you must be a student of classroom management. You have to put in the time to learn the strategies that really work and understand how they relate to one another. A semi-understanding of classroom management won't do. In fact, it will likely make you worse off.

YES, YOU CAN

It isn't always easy to have a positive attitude about teaching when seemingly everyone around you, including your closest teacher chums, think you're off your rocker—or at least, naive. But the truth is, they're wrong. There are scores of teachers all over the world, some in the most difficult circumstances imaginable, who this very minute are enjoying the teaching experience they've always wanted. You can too.

You really can create a classroom your students love being part of and you love teaching. You really can provide a safe haven from the raging storms outside your classroom door. You really can bestow inspiration, love, and lessons that last a lifetime.

But you have to think differently than most. You have to go your own way. You have to ignore the cacophony of voices that say you can't do it. You have to box up all those self-defeating thoughts and negative attitudes bouncing around in your head and carry them out to the school dumpster— saying goodbye forever.

There is a lot at stake.

So much is on the line.

And your students are counting on you.

For more strategies, tips, and solutions,

visit smartclassroommanagement.com

Made in the USA
Las Vegas, NV
31 May 2022

49610507R00114